CBS NEWS

EDITED BY IAN JACKMAN

INTRODUCTION BY DAN RATHER

RONALD REAGAN
REMEMBERED

SIMON & SCHUSTER   NEW YORK   LONDON   TORONTO   SYDNEY

Simon & Schuster
Rockefeller Center
1230 Avenue of the Americas
New York, NY 10020

SIMON & SCHUSTER and colophon are registered trademarks
of Simon & Schuster, Inc.

For information regarding special discounts for bulk purchases,
please contact Simon & Schuster Special Sales at 1-800-456-6798
or business@simonandschuster.com

Designed by Joel Avirom and Jason Snyder
Design assistant Meghan Day Healey

Manufactured in the United States of America

10 9 8 7 6 5 4 3 2 1

Library of Congress Cataloging-in-Publication Data
Ronald Reagan remembered : CBS News / edited by Ian Jackman, introduction by Dan Rather.
p. cm
1. Reagan, Ronald. 2. Reagan, Ronald—Death and burial. 3. Presidents—United States—Biography.
I. Jackman, Ian. II. Columbia Broadcasting System, Inc.
E877.R665 2004
973.927'092—dc22
[B]   2004058990

ISBN 0-7432-7153-X

CBS Worldwide gratefully acknowledges permission from the following sources to reprint material in their control:

Patti Davis, Copyright © 2004/*People* Magazine. "Waiting . . . and the End," by Patti Davis.

Los Angeles Times, Copyright © 2004. "Farewell to a President," by Steve Chawkins. "Farewell to a President," by Fay Fiore, Vicki Kemper, and Daryl Kelly. "Ronald Wilson Reagan, 1911–2004," by Johanna Neuman.

Newsweek, June 14, 2004. Copyright © 2004 Newsweek, Inc. All rights reserved. "American Dreamer," by Jon Meacham.

The New York Times Co., Copyright © 2004. "Legacy of Reagan Now Begins the Test of Time," by R. W. Apple, Jr.

The Philadelphia Inquirer, Copyright © 2004. "For Thousands in Line, Personal Farewells," by Ron Hutcheson.

Time Inc., Copyright © 2004. "How His Legacy Lives On," by Richard Lacayo and John F. Dickerson.

The Washington Post Writers Group, Copyright © 2004. "A Paradox," by Richard Cohen.

All photos courtesy AP/Wide World photos except pp. x, 12–13, 23, 32–33, 49, 76–77, 95, 101, 105, 108, 125, 167, 169 (top), 171, 176, which are courtesy of the Ronald Reagan Presidential Library.

CONTENTS

TIMELINE

February 6, 1911	Born in Tampico, Illinois, to Nelle Wilson and John Edward ("Jack") Reagan.
1920	Moves to Dixon, Illinois.
1926	First of six summers working as lifeguard at Lowell Park, Dixon.
June 1928	Graduates from Dixon High School.
1928–1932	Attends Eureka College, Eureka, Illinois.
December 1932	Works as announcer at WOC radio in Davenport, Iowa.
April 1933	Moves to Des Moines as announcer for WHO radio.
April 20, 1937	Signs for Warner Bros. after screen test.
May	Appointed second lieutenant in the Officers' Reserve Corps of the Cavalry, U.S. Army.
June	Begins first motion picture, *Love is on the Air*.
January 26, 1940	Marries Jane Wyman.
September	Plays George Gipp in *Knute Rockne—All American*.
January 4, 1941	Maureen Reagan born.
April 1942	Called to active duty and assigned to the First Motion Picture Unit of the Army Air Corps in Culver City, California.
January 1943	Promoted to first lieutenant.
July	Promoted to captain.
March 18, 1945	Michael Reagan born.
December	Discharged from the army.
March 1947	Elected president of the Screen Actors Guild.
October	Testifies before the House Un-American Activities Committee.
June 28, 1949	Reagan and Jane Wyman divorce finalized.
March 4, 1952	Marries Nancy Davis.
October 22	Patricia Davis born.
September 1954	First appearance on *GE Theater*.
May 28, 1958	Ronald Prescott Reagan born.
July 1960	Reagan resigns as president of the Screen Actors Guild.
August 1962	Last appearance on *GE Theater*.
1964	Makes last movie, *The Killers*, and becomes host of *Death Valley Days*.
October 27	"A Time for Choosing," speech for Barry Goldwater, launches political career.
1965	Publication of autobiography, *Where's the Rest of Me?*
November 8, 1966	Defeats Edmund G. "Pat" Brown in election for governor of California.
January 2, 1967	Inaugurated as governor of California.
August 1968	Announces candidacy for president.
November 1970	Wins reelection for governor, beating Jesse M. Unruh, speaker of the state assembly.
1971	Signs the California Welfare Reform Act.

November 1975	Announces candidacy for president for the 1976 election.
August 19, 1976	Addresses Republican National Convention in Kansas City.
November 1979	Announces candidacy for the Republican presidential nomination.
July 17, 1980	Accepts nomination at Republican National Convention in Detroit and selects George H. W. Bush as vice presidential candidate.
November 4	Ronald Reagan elected the fortieth president of the United States.
January 20, 1981	Takes oath of office and gives inaugural address.
March 30	President Reagan and three others shot by John W. Hinckley, Jr., outside the Washington Hilton.
July	Nominates the first woman Supreme Court justice, Sandra Day O'Connor.
August	Signs the Economic Recovery Tax Act and fires striking federal air traffic controllers.
March 1983	Gives "evil empire" speech and proposes Strategic Defense Initiative.
October	Truck bomb kills 241 U.S. Marines in Beirut. Orders invasion of Grenada.
November 1984	Wins reelection, defeating Walter F. Mondale with 525 electoral college votes.
January 21, 1985	Second inaugural.
July	Undergoes colon cancer surgery.
November	Meets Mikhail Gorbachev for first time in Geneva.
January 28, 1986	Space shuttle *Challenger* explodes.
April	United States bombs two sites in Libya.
October	Reykjavik summit with President Gorbachev.
January 1987	Undergoes prostate surgery.
May 17	Iraqi missile hits USS *Stark*, killing thirty-seven.
June 12	Gives Brandenburg Gate speech.
December 8	Signs Intermediate Nuclear Force (INF) Treaty with Mikhail Gorbachev.
May–June 1988	Moscow summit.
January 20, 1989	President Reagan leaves the White House.
June 14	Receives honorary knighthood from Queen Elizabeth II.
September	Has surgery to remove fluid from brain.
February 1990	Begins videotaped testimony in trial of Iran-contra figure John Poindexter.
February 6, 1991	Celebrates eightieth birthday at the Beverly Hilton Hotel, Beverly Hills.
November 4	Dedication of the Ronald Reagan Library and Center for Public Affairs, Simi Valley, California.
May 1992	Presents the first Ronald Reagan Freedom Award to Mikhail Gorbachev.
November 5, 1994	Publishes letter announcing that he has Alzheimer's disease.
August 2001	Daughter Maureen dies, age sixty.
June 5, 2004	Dies at home in Bel Air, California.

INTRODUCTION

by Dan Rather

Though the twenty-first century is not yet a decade old, the twentieth century already seems a distant memory. Because of this sense of remove, we may now be able to appreciate, in a way that we could not at the end of his second term, just how completely Ronald Reagan embodied what is called "the American century." Born in 1911, he held memories that few alive today can claim. The small-town America about which President Reagan would often wax nostalgic was not a rhetorical fabrication; it was the reality that young Ronald Reagan knew as a boy. He came of age during the Great Depression and served with the Army Air Force Motion Picture Unit during World War II. He acted on the silver screen during Hollywood's golden age. Amid the strife of the 1960s, he was the governor of California known for locking horns with antiwar protestors.

Ronald Reagan was a man who was fully a part of the era in which he lived, an era that left an indelible stamp on the American culture and psyche. By the time Reagan was elected president, his understanding of this country and its major currents of thought and feeling was innate. Even if one discounts all his considerable rhetorical skill, President Reagan did not have to reach to connect with his fellow Americans: if the times really do make the man, President Reagan was as American as they come.

This quality may well have been at the heart of President Reagan's political success, the substance that informed his considerable blessings of easy communication. Many have called President Reagan the Great Communicator, and the label sometimes grates on his partisans, who see in it a reluctance to credit the Reagan ideology. But to Reagan detractors and defenders alike, one might ask: Just what is leadership, in a democracy, but the harnessing of policy to the horse of persuasion? In a successful presidency, these realms are inseparable, and this was something that President Reagan always seemed to grasp.

An official portrait of President Reagan, 1981.

In the public role of the presidency, Ronald Reagan knew how to personify the American spirit of the times, and reflect it back to an American public that generally liked what it saw. He spoke to an elevated sense of the American self, and he did so convincingly, in language that carried neither a self-conscious populist pose nor a high academic gloss. To recall President Reagan's speeches—his first inaugural, his eulogizing of the *Challenger* crew, his farewell address—is to remember a time not so long ago when words still reached out to the American imagination. Today's focus group–tested soundbites pale by comparison.

For many Americans, for many Republicans and Democrats alike, Ronald Reagan holds a privileged place in America's recent historical landscape. And in this presidential election year, no sooner had President Reagan left us than each major-party candidate sought to lay claim to his legacy: one through ideological and policy affinities, the other on the issue of federal funding for stem-cell research for treating Alzheimer's and other neurological diseases.

On June 11, 2004, as the sun set over the American continent, a nation said its last good-byes to Ronald Wilson Reagan, fortieth president of the United States. On a California hillside facing the Pacific Ocean, a site rich in symbolism for a onetime movie star and two-term governor of the Golden State, President Reagan's remarkable journey came to its end, with history trailing in its wake.

In the preceding days, America had witnessed a state funeral in the nation's capital, a rite this country had not seen in a generation. As the caisson bearing President Reagan's casket made its way past the many thousands who lined Pennsylvania and Constitution avenues, a certain air of triumph mingled with the solemnity of the occasion. As President Bush would say in the eulogy he delivered at the National Cathedral, America had lost Ronald Reagan only days before, but we had "missed him for a long time." Those who lined the streets had come not only to pay their respects but also to celebrate a life long lived, and one released at last from the terrible hold of Alzheimer's disease.

Those of us in the news media who had come to Washington to cover the funeral of a president tried, with the help of historians, biographers, and President Reagan's political contemporaries, to come to terms with his legacy.

Much was said, of course, about Reagan's role in bringing about the collapse of the Soviet Union and the end of the cold war. Ubiquitous, too, was the word "optimism," used to describe the trait that, for so many, defined Reagan's personality and presidential vision. We heard about the Reagan wit and gift for oratory, and his easy way of connecting with his—as we can still hear him say in that trademark, mellifluous voice—"fellow Americans."

But it was an observation made by Edmund Morris, President Reagan's official biographer, that may have best made sense of Ronald Reagan the man and the president, and best encapsulated what he had meant to his country and to the world. Mr. Morris recalled that former French president François Mitterrand had once said, roughly translated, that Reagan "Truly had a notion of the state." Former Canadian Prime Minister Brian Mulroney, who eulogized President Reagan, also picked up on Mitterrand's words, elaborating that Reagan understood "that there is a vast difference between the job of president and the role of president." The journalist Lou Cannon, who had covered the Reagan White House for *The Washington Post*, expressed a parallel thought: "The greatness of Reagan was not that he was in America, but that America was inside of him," he said, recasting something that Walter Lippmann had once said of Mitterrand's predecessor, de Gaulle.

Given the current international climate, it may seem odd verging on blasphemous to use one French leader or the words of another as a yardstick for evaluating one of our own. But in the post–World War II years, General de Gaulle was, like Winston Churchill and Franklin Roosevelt during the war, a man whose name had become virtually synonymous with that of his nation. In the 1980s, at the late height of the cold war, Ronald Reagan achieved a similar level of identification with the United States of America.

This was true for those who watched the United States from afar, from Western and Eastern Europe and from South America; and it was true, also, for political observers and everyday Americans here at home. It was true for those who admired President Reagan's willingness to confront the Soviet Union and it was true for those dismayed by his administration's interventions in Latin America. It was true for those who approved of the deregulation and tax-cutting that marked his economic policies, and it was true, too, for those who saw in the 1980s a decade of rapaciousness and greed. No matter where you stood, the nation and the time bore the unmistakable imprimatur of Ronald Reagan.

The public makes its opinions known instantly. American voters made their judgments on President Reagan known in the landslide election result of 1984, and the American heart did so again with a resounding outpouring upon Ronald Reagan's death earlier this year. History, however, is slower to register its verdicts. In these politically charged times, pundits and prognosticators of all stripes would have us believe that we can know how the future will treat our shared past, and that we can know it *now*. But real historians, schooled as they are in the shifting tides of fortune, tell us that true historical assessments can take generations to render.

In these pages and in the accompanying DVD, CBS News has brought together writings about and images of Ronald Reagan's life and presidency. This will by no means be the last word on President Reagan and on what he meant to the United States and the world, but it is meant to provide an enduring remembrance of an important American, of the times in which he lived and of the history he helped to shape. Here is a record of presidential triumphs and trials, of a public career that spanned much of the twentieth century. Here are pictures and events that you may remember well, or that the younger among you may be encountering for the first time.

From small-town Illinois to Hollywood, from the White House and, now, back to his beloved California, Ronald Wilson Reagan's journey was indeed remarkable, and uniquely American. We at CBS News hope that you will enjoy and learn from this collection of snapshots from the long road he traveled.

—*Dan Rather*
New York, 2004

RONALD REAGAN
REMEMBERED

PART ONE

RONALD WILSON REAGAN

Los Angeles Times, June 6, 2004

Ronald Wilson Reagan
1911–2004

by *Johanna Neuman*, Times *Staff Writer*

Ronald Reagan, the Hollywood actor who became one of the most popular presidents of the twentieth century and transformed the political landscape of an era with his vision of conservative government, died Saturday at his home in the Bel Air neighborhood of Los Angeles. He was ninety-three.

His wife, Nancy, his greatest fan and fierce protector, was at his side. For ten years, he suffered from Alzheimer's, an incapacitating brain disease. In 1994, he bade a poignant farewell to "my fellow Americans." In a handwritten letter, made public by his office, he said he was setting out on "the journey that will lead me into the sunset of my life."

In a statement relayed by chief of staff Joanne Drake, who represents the family, Nancy Reagan said: "My family and I would like the world to know that President Ronald Reagan has passed away.... We appreciate everyone's prayers." Drake said Reagan's death came at 1:00 P.M. and was caused by pneumonia, complicated by Alzheimer's.

The disease robbed Reagan of his ability to remember much of his own remarkable history: that he had served eight years as governor of California and eight more as president of the United States, and that he had led America's politics rightward toward the middle. Only one Democrat has succeeded him: Bill Clinton, a "new Democrat," who did as much or more to achieve such conservative goals as balancing the federal budget and changing welfare than anything Reagan himself accomplished.

Reagan inspired a missionary corps of conservatives who hold countless elected offices and government jobs to this day. Others have been elected since he left the White House. Indeed, biographer Lou Cannon likened the Reagan revolution to a time bomb, citing political analyst Michael Barone's tally showing that more Reagan Republicans won congressional seats in 1994 than they did when he was president. Even in his final years, he was a role model. President George W. Bush, who tugged the country even farther right, has called Reagan "a hero in the American story."

As recently as last month, Nancy Reagan had said her husband's disease was worsening. "Ronnie's long journey has finally taken him to a distant place where I can no longer reach him," she said. When he died, she and Reagan's son and daughter Ronald Prescott Reagan and Patti Davis were at the family home, chief of staff Drake said. She said son Michael Reagan arrived a short time later. He had spent all day Friday with his father.

Reagan's death brought accolades and condolences from around the world. President George W. Bush was told of his death while visiting Paris to mark the anniversary of D-day. "It's a sad hour in the life of America," Bush said, adding that Reagan "leaves behind a nation he restored and a world he helped save." Former British prime minister Margaret Thatcher, Reagan's contemporary and political ally, declared that "millions of men and women . . . live in freedom today because of the policies he pursued."

Former presidents offered statements of praise. Gerald R. Ford called Reagan "an excellent leader of our nation during challenging times." Bill Clinton said, "He personified the indomitable optimism of the American people . . . [and kept] America at the forefront of the fight for freedom." George H. W. Bush said, "We had been political opponents and became close friends. He could take a stand . . . and do it without creating bitterness."

In California, Governor Arnold Schwarzenegger called Reagan "a great American patriot" and said, "He was a hero to me."

World and national leaders were expected to gather at the National Cathedral in Washington for Reagan's funeral, after his body lies in state for two days at the Reagan presidential library and museum near Simi Valley, and then for two days in Washington at the Capitol Rotunda. Then the body was to be returned to the presidential library for private burial. Details of the arrangements were not final.

Optimism Was Catching

As the nation's fortieth president, Reagan left lasting contributions to the world, his nation and the people he served. Graced with a gift for story-telling, a ready wit and a visceral understanding of the aspirations of his countrymen, Reagan had the rare distinction of leaving office more popular than when he arrived.

Part of his gift was his ability to make Americans, shaken by the Vietnam War and the scandal of Watergate, feel good about themselves. His optimism was real and unyielding. Once, after surgery for colon cancer, he told reporters: "I didn't have cancer. I had something inside of me that had cancer in it, and it was removed." It helped that he was an actor. "There have been times in this office," he once told interviewer David Brinkley, "when I've wondered how you could do the job if you hadn't been an actor."

People called him the Gipper, because he played Notre Dame football star George Gipp in the 1940 movie *Knute Rockne—All American*. On his deathbed, Gipp urges Coach Rockne to implore the Fighting Irish to "win one for the Gipper." As president, Reagan urged his fellow Americans to do the same, time and again: to write Congress for tax relief, to vote Republican—so they, too, could win one for the Gipper.

People also called him the Great Communicator, because he understood the presidency was a pulpit, and he used it to preach. Mostly his sermons were about a

Screen actor Ronald Reagan as Notre Dame football player George Gipp ("The Gipper") in *Knute Rockne—All American*. The 1940 film about the legendary coach gave Reagan his best-known screen role.

simple kind of conservatism: cut taxes so investments of the wealthy would trickle down to the poor; build America's military might so world communism would topple and fall. "Mr. Gorbachev," he shouted, at the Brandenburg Gate in Berlin during a visit in June 1987, "tear down this wall!"

Ten years later, after the Berlin Wall had tumbled and the Soviet empire collapsed, Reagan was strolling in Armand Hammer Park near his home. The Toledo *Blade* reported that a Ukrainian from Ohio and his twelve-year-old grandson asked if Reagan would sit on a park bench with the boy for a picture. He obliged. The grandfather later told *The New York Times* that they had thanked him for opposing communism.

Yes, Reagan replied, that had been his job.

PLUSES AND MINUSES

Reagan left a tangled legacy.

He presided over a historic agreement to ban intermediate range nuclear missiles with the Soviet Union, which he had reviled as an "evil empire." But he also presided over a debacle in Lebanon with uncounted victims, including 241 U.S. troops, mostly Marines; and he presided over the Iran-contra affair, a scandal that severely damaged his administration.

Reagan's tenure produced lower inflation, interest rates and unemployment. But his term also saw a busted budget and record deficits, which made America a net importer and tripled the national debt. It "mortgaged much of our future vitality," said conservative columnist George F. Will. Nearly fifteen years passed before the nation was able to post a surplus.

The president himself was a man of striking contradictions, say Jane Mayer, a *New Yorker* magazine staff writer, and Doyle McManus, the *Times'* Washington bureau chief, in their book, *Landslide: The Unmaking of the President, 1984–1988.* He was a gifted leader, they write, but he could be detached and indecisive. He was an overwhelmingly popular politician, they say, but he could be shy and intensely private and kept a personal distance from almost everyone except his wife, Nancy.

"On balance, Reagan was a strong man, but an extraordinarily weak manager," biographer Cannon said in his book *President Reagan: The Role of a Lifetime.* He restored public confidence in the presidency, Cannon wrote,

"without mastering the difficult art of wielding presidential power." Reagan often said: "Government is not the solution to our problems. Government is the problem." In fact, Cannon said, "Reagan thought so little of government that he did not think enough about it." As a result, he treated the presidency with a hands-off style of management that tested the abilities of those charged to run the executive branch, sometimes with unhappy results.

During a stop-off en route to an economic summit in Tokyo in 1986, the Gipper shows good throwing form as the president and first lady take a stroll on the beach in Honolulu, Hawaii.

But he also could be a very personal president. He shared jellybeans from a jar in the Oval Office. A recent collection, *Reagan: A Life in Letters*, revealed that he handwrote an astonishing assortment of notes to friends, adversaries, world leaders and plain folks, from Soviet leader Leonid Brezhnev to a seventh-grader who requested federal help because his mother had declared his bedroom a disaster area. Reagan's letters asked whether governments truly reflected the needs of their people, told of his imaginings about a ballistic missile defense system and suggested, with a fatherly chuckle, that the youngster volunteer to clean up his room himself.

Many Americans saw in him things they also wanted to believe about themselves, said cultural historian Garry Wills, in his book *Reagan's America: Innocents at Home.* They were convinced, Wills wrote, that both he and they were hopeful and independent, strong and God-fearing, as well as destined to be extraordinary. They shaped their faith in him and in themselves to accommodate any uncomfortable realities, Wills said, and they ignored his inconsistencies.

This helped to shield Reagan from political disapproval. Confounding opponents, he seemed at times to be immune to controversy. "The Teflon-coated presidency," complained former congresswoman Patricia Schroeder (D-Colo.), when criticisms would not take hold, but slipped off instead like grease on a nonstick frying pan.

Reagan was protected, too, by his style. He did not turn political foes into personal enemies. House Speaker Thomas P. "Tip" O'Neill, an earthy populist from Boston who championed liberal causes with a fervor to match Reagan's devotion to conservative crusades, often went from Capitol Hill down to the White House at the end of the day for a quiet chat between two Irish pols.

"There's just something about the guy that people like," O'Neill once explained to *The Washington Post.* "They're rooting for him, and of course they're rooting for him because we haven't had any presidential successes for years—Kennedy killed, Johnson with Vietnam, Nixon with Watergate, Ford, Carter and all the rest." O'Neill remembered how Reagan would say to him, "Tip, you and I are political enemies only until six o'clock. It's four o'clock now. Can we pretend that it's six o'clock?"

Finally, Reagan was sustained by his sense of humor, which he often exercised in times of adversity. When a would-be assassin gunned him down outside a Washington hotel during the third month of his presidency, he quipped to a doctor laboring to save his life: "I hope you're a Republican."

As in "win one for the Gipper," when Reagan did not have a good line of his own, he borrowed one from a movie in which he had appeared, or which he especially liked. To Reagan, the presidency was often the stage for a well-rehearsed script. He tapped the talents of a stable of writers, including the eloquent Peggy Noonan.

On the fortieth anniversary of D-day, she provided his tribute on the palisades of Normandy to American veterans who had flown to France for the occasion. "These are the boys of Pointe du Hoc," he intoned, his delivery a marvel of dramatic narrative and pauses at the punch lines. "These are the men who took the cliffs. These are the champions who helped free a continent. These are the heroes who helped win a war."

Veterans cried, said *The Washington Post*, adding that he had moved "even reporters and Democrats to tears."

His writers knew history. Left to himself, Reagan sometimes garbled it. This mattered little, however, because he had perfect pitch for its music. "Reagan would embody great chunks of the American experience, become deeply involved with them emotionally, while having only the haziest notion of what really occurred," Wills says. "He had a skill for striking 'historical' attitudes combined with a striking lack of historical attention."

What he was doing was acting, but it served him well, even in times of trouble. Alexander M. Haig caused a stir, for example, by resigning abruptly as secretary of state after battling the White House staff and embarrassing the administration with an emotional pronouncement following the assassination attempt that "I am in control here."

As Reagan prepared to answer questions from reporters about Haig's departure, he regaled his aides with jokes. Chief of Staff James A. Baker cautioned against levity at serious moments.

"Don't worry, Jim," Reagan replied. "I'll play it somber."

And he did.

"These are the boys of Pointe du Hoc." During the celebrations in 1984 marking the fortieth anniversary of D-day, President Reagan speaks at the U.S. Ranger Monument at Pointe du Hoc, Normandy.

SMALL-TOWN ROOTS

Ronald Wilson Reagan was born February 6, 1911, in Tampico, Illinois, the second son of John Edward Reagan and Nelle Wilson Reagan.

His father, an Irish-Catholic Democrat, was a shoe salesman and charming storyteller, but he had a restless spirit and a drinking problem. In the early years of Reagan's childhood, his father had difficulty holding a job.

The Reagans moved from one small town to another in rural Illinois. For a brief period, they resided on the South Side of Chicago. By the age of eight, he had lived in seven homes. In 1920, when Reagan was nine, the family settled down at last in the small community of Dixon, about a hundred miles due west of Chicago.

Dixon was where Reagan went to high school, played football and fell in love with a preacher's daughter. It was where he took up his famous duties as a lifeguard in Lowell Park, northeast of town on the Rock River. He was credited with saving seventy-seven lives.

He was "Dutch" Reagan then, a nickname given to him when he was a baby by his father, who thought he looked like "a fat little Dutchman." Reagan preferred "Dutch" to Ronald, which he considered not manly.

His mother was a pious woman who had a big influence on her sons, Neil and Ronald. Cheerful and energetic, she taught that people were innately good and could achieve great things with perseverance. She gave Ronald his first taste of acting: playing parts in moralistic church skits, some of which she wrote.

By contrast, in an early autobiography, *Where's the Rest of Me? The Ronald Reagan Story*, he described coming home to find his father "flat on his back on the front porch and no one there to lend a hand but me. He was drunk, dead to the world. I wanted to let myself in the house and go to bed and pretend he wasn't there." Instead, the scrawny eleven-year-old tugged his father inside and put him to bed.

Reagan said that he felt no resentment and credited his mother. "She told Neil and myself over and over that alcoholism was a sickness—that we should love and help our father and never condemn him for something that was beyond his control."

The family of John E. ("Jack") and Nelle Reagan in Tampico, Illinois, around 1913. Standing between young Ronald and his father is the future president's older brother Neil.

"Dutch" Reagan, lifeguard on the Rock River over six summers, pictured in 1931.

But it scarred him: As a youngster, he tried to avoid the trouble that alcoholism caused at home; as an adult, Cannon said, sometimes he could not bring himself to confront the trouble that infighting caused on his White House staff.

After high school, Reagan enrolled in Eureka College, a small Christian school twenty-one miles east of Peoria. Early on, he found his public voice. The college president, under fire for restrictions against smoking, dancing and staying out after 9:30 P.M., compounded his problems by threatening to eliminate courses and fire teachers to save money.

Reagan, the freshman representative, was asked to speak on behalf of students who were in revolt. "He did not call for a return to law and order or ask the students to protest to the trustees through established channels," writes Bill Boyarsky, a retired *Times* city editor, political writer and columnist, in his book, *Ronald Reagan: His Life and Rise to the Presidency*. Nor did he criticize the faculty for supporting the students, as he did during student unrest when he was the governor of California.

Instead, Boyarsky says, "he offered a resolution calling for a student strike." Reagan's emotional appeal prevailed: All but a few students refused to attend classes. Ultimately, the president of Eureka College resigned.

In his autobiography, Reagan said he discovered while he was making his strike speech "that an audience has a feel to it, and, in the parlance of the theater, the audience and I were together. . . . It was heady wine."

When he graduated from Eureka in 1932, the nation was deep in the Depression. "We didn't live on the wrong side of the railroad tracks," Reagan said later about those meager years, "but we lived so close to them we could hear the whistle real loud."

Sportscaster Reagan working at the microphone for the WHO radio station in Des Moines in 1937.

Even in the depths of the nation's economic catastrophe, Reagan was determined to succeed. He wanted to be a broadcaster. He was attracted to radio partly by the new president, Franklin Delano Roosevelt. Memorizing portions of FDR's first inaugural address, Reagan later echoed Roosevelt's cadence. As for FDR's New Deal politics, "I was a near-hopeless hemophilic liberal." Reagan wrote later. "I bled for 'causes.'"

He landed a part-time announcer's job at WOC in Davenport, Iowa. Within a year, WOC had merged with its big-sister station, WHO in Des Moines, and Reagan was hired as a sports announcer and re-created Chicago Cubs games.

On assignment for WHO covering Chicago Cubs spring training, Reagan takes a screen test at the Warner Bros. studio in Hollywood.

Reagan often told a story during his presidency of how he would get abbreviated information about a game in progress by telegraph and relay it to listeners as if he were describing the action. Except once, when the ticker died.

"When the [telegraph] slip came through, it said, 'The wire's gone dead.' Well, I had the ball on the way to the plate," Reagan recalled to a group of baseball players at a Hall of Fame lunch at the White House in 1981. "So I had Billy [Jurges] foul one off. . . . And I had him foul one back at third base and described the fight between the two kids who were trying to get to the ball. Then I had him foul one that just missed being a home run." Finally, with Reagan sweating and listeners wondering about this odd succession of foul balls, the ticker started to click again.

"And the slip came through the window, and I could hardly talk for laughing," Reagan recalled. "It said, 'Jurges popped out on the first pitch.'"

Radio loved Reagan's voice, but he longed to be an actor. WHO sent him to Catalina Island in 1937 to cover the Cubs during spring training. While he was in California, he wrangled a screen test and signed a contract for $200 a week with Warner Bros. studio.

PRIVATE AND PUBLIC TRANSITION

Reagan acted in fifty-two movies cast as a good guy and in one made-for-TV film, *The Killers*, cast as a villain. He later said he regretted making the picture. It was considered too violent for television and was released in theaters just as his political career began.

In 1940, he married actress Jane Wyman, and they appeared together in a sequel to their first pairing in *Brother Rat*. It was called *Brother Rat and a Baby*. Within a year, their first child was born, a daughter they named Maureen Elizabeth. Later they adopted a son, Michael Edward. Their daughter died in August 2001 of melanoma. She was sixty.

Reagan's big movie break came with *Knute Rockne—All American*, the film that immortalized the Gipper. But his most challenging part came in *Kings Row*, a 1942 picture in which he played a small-town playboy whose legs are needlessly amputated by a vicious surgeon. Both he and critics called it his best performance.

He became a board member of the Screen Actors Guild. Stars who commanded big money—Robert Montgomery, Cary Grant, James Cagney—welcomed him as an equal.

Reagan's film career was sidetracked by World War II, and it never recovered. Disqualified from combat because he was nearsighted, he was sent to the First Motion Picture Unit of the Army Air Forces in suburban Culver City, which made over four hundred training films. He was discharged on December 9, 1945, as a captain.

His involvement with the Screen Actors Guild increased, and with it a growing interest in public life, which Wyman complained took all his time. In 1948, their marriage—to Reagan's painful surprise—headed for divorce. It was for him a personal trauma. "The plain truth was," he said, "that such a thing was so far from even being imagined by me that I had no resources to call upon."

The trauma coincided with his first stirrings of conservatism. He remained a Democrat, urging Dwight D. Eisenhower to run for president as a Democrat and campaigning for Helen Gahagan Douglas in her futile U.S. Senate race against Richard M. Nixon. It would not be until the early 1960s that he switched parties. "I didn't leave the Democratic Party," he said. "The party left me."

By 1947, Reagan had become president of the Screen Actors Guild. He was swept up in ideological turmoil that tormented Hollywood. The House Un-American Activities Committee began investigating claims of communist influence within the studios. Writers and actors were blacklisted. Some never worked again.

Reagan was convinced that communists intended to seize control of the movie industry so it could be used as "a worldwide propaganda base." The remedy, he wrote in *Where's the Rest of Me?*, was "that each American generation must be re-educated to the precariousness of liberty."

Reagan and other actors appeared before HUAC to testify to their opposition to communism. They "lent [their] names" to the luster of its hearings, say Larry Ceplair and Steven Englund in their book, *The Inquisition in Hollywood*.

Actor and president of the Screen Actors Guild Ronald Reagan testifies before the House Committee on Un-American Activities (HUAC) in Washington, October 1947. HUAC was investigating alleged communist activities in the movie industry.

In 1952, he married Nancy Davis, a young actress whose mother, Edith Luckett, had been on stage and whose stepfather, Dr. Loyal Davis, was a prominent neurosurgeon. She gave up acting to devote herself to her husband. They had two children, Patricia Ann and Ronald Prescott.

For Reagan, there was comfort in having a family again.

Enter General Electric, stage right. For eight years, beginning in 1954, Reagan served GE as the host of a televised series of dramas. He also was its goodwill ambassador to employees and to civic and business groups around the country. While his motive was to make money, over time the experience of speaking to business people helped crystallize his views and prepared him for active politics.

His talks, initially only lighthearted reminiscences of Hollywood's golden age, began to grow more serious. In speeches with titles like "Encroaching Government Controls" and "Our Eroding Freedoms," he broadened his scope to include a wide range of national issues. At first, he confined his deepest political beliefs to private communications—a 1960 letter to Vice President Richard M. Nixon, for instance, in which he said of John F. Kennedy: "Under the tousled boyish haircut is still old Karl Marx."

By 1962, his speeches had become more political—and more controversial. Under pressure, General Electric ended the arrangement. He had become so popular, he said, that at least three years of bookings had to be canceled.

"It would be nice to accept this as a tribute to my oratory," Reagan later wrote. "But I think the real reason had to do with a change that was taking place all over America. People wanted to talk about and hear about encroaching government control. And hopefully they wanted suggestions as to what they themselves could do to turn the tide."

With Marilyn Monroe in Los Angeles, 1959.

MOVING TO WORLD STAGE

Reagan's political fortunes rose from the ashes of Republican presidential nominee Barry Goldwater's spectacular defeat in 1964. Reagan offered a friendly antidote to Goldwater's strident rhetoric. Reagan's tone suggested patriotic concern and continuity with the past. Unlike Goldwater, he could sell conservatism with a smile.

In a fund-raising address televised to the nation, Reagan honed "the speech," as it was known during his GE days, into a clarion call. Americans saw the smoothest, most articulate, most attractive champion of the Republican cause in a generation. Biographer Bill Boyarsky says Reagan's speech, "A Time for Choosing," stirred conservatives just as William Jennings Bryan's "Cross of Gold" speech had electrified farmers and factory workers in 1896.

Goldwater lost to Lyndon Johnson, but Reagan won national acclaim.

The next spring, Holmes P. Tuttle, a wealthy Los Angeles car dealer who had promoted the fund-raising speech, invited other millionaires to support Reagan in a race for governor of California. The millionaires, later known as Reagan's "kitchen Cabinet," hired the California campaign management team of Stuart Spencer and Bill Roberts. They, in turn, hired professors to brief Reagan on state issues and broaden his command of literary allusions.

His years on television for GE, then as host of *Death Valley Days*, had made Reagan a familiar face. But it brought criticism as well. Democrats derided him as a puppet who mouthed words scripted by others. In *An American Life*, a later autobiography, he recalled that incumbent governor Edmund G. "Pat" Brown aired an ad in which he told schoolchildren, "I'm running against an actor," then added, "and you know who killed Lincoln, don't you?"

Reagan, for his part, gave versions of "the speech" at every opportunity. He argued that government was too big, taxes were too high and regulation was strangling business. Often he ended with "*Ya basta!*" It was Spanish for "Enough, already!"

Californians said yes, overwhelmingly.

Reagan defeated Brown by nearly one million votes and swept Republicans into every major executive office except attorney general.

During his eight years in Sacramento, Reagan's performance foreshadowed his stewardship in Washington. Against Democratic majorities among lawmakers for most of the time in both places, he portrayed himself as a "citizen politician" determined to "squeeze, cut and trim" and get government off "the backs of its people."

The champion of striking students at Eureka College vowed to restore order at protest-torn campuses throughout California and was pleased to see the firing of nationally respected University of California president Clark Kerr. Reagan also supported the first-ever UC student tuition.

He appointed a former member of the John Birch Society to head his Office of Economic Opportunity and to campaign against legal assistance for the rural poor. In a compromise, Boyarsky writes, he gave up a permanent ceiling on welfare appropriations, but he succeeded in reducing welfare rolls.

Squeezing, cutting and trimming government were harder. In his first year, he proposed slashing the state budget by an unprecedented 10 percent—but ended up signing a spending program 10 percent larger than his predecessor's. He kept proclaiming "squeeze, cut and trim," but his budgets, hammered by inflation, ballooned from his first of $4.6 billion to his last of $10.2 billion. He signed what at the time was the biggest state tax increase in the nation's history: $844 million in the first year, $1.01 billion in the second. It marked the first of a roller-coaster series of tax increases and rebates.

One of his most remarkable flip-flops involved his opposition to payroll withholding of state income taxes. "My feet are in concrete," he said, over and over. But in 1970, when the state faced a serious cash flow crisis, Reagan finally gave in. "That sound you hear," he told reporters, "is the concrete breaking around my feet." That same year he found himself in a personal controversy. He had paid no state income tax himself because of "business reverses."

As he campaigned, he had been dismissive of some environmental concerns. "You know, a tree is a tree," he said. "How many more do you need to look at?" But as governor, he signed some of the nation's strictest air and water quality laws, increased state parkland and started requiring environmental impact reports on state construction projects.

He signed a historic abortion reform bill authored by a Democrat that vastly liberalized the procedure in California. Advocates promoted it as a

model for other states. Later, as a national political figure, Reagan would hold the support of the most militant antiabortionists, while doing relatively little to advance their cause.

"Reagan was not as good as the Republicans like to think, or as bad as the Democrats would have you believe," declared Democratic Assembly Speaker Jesse M. Unruh, who had opposed him unsuccessfully when he ran for a second term.

Reagan's march on Washington began almost as soon as he reached the state capitol. He ran for president in 1968, but fell to Nixon. By 1975, when Reagan completed his second term as governor, Nixon had resigned in dis-

California Justice Marshall F. McCombs swears in Ronald Reagan as governor of California, Sacramento, January 2, 1967.

grace. Reagan began an all-out, two-year drive to wrest the 1976 nomination from incumbent Gerald R. Ford, an appointed vice president who became president on the resignation of Nixon. Reagan fell short by a handful of delegates to the Republican national convention.

But Ford lost to Jimmy Carter, and Reagan became the front-runner to challenge Carter in 1980. This time Reagan was not to be denied. He flirted with asking former President Ford to be his running mate, but negotiations faltered—so he turned to George Bush, who in the primaries had called his fiscal policy "voodoo economics." By 1983, Reagan vowed, he would cut taxes, boost defense spending and balance the budget.

Under Carter, Americans had been battered by double-digit inflation, stagnant growth and a fuel shortage that caused long lines at gasoline stations. They had been humiliated by the imprisonment of fifty-two Americans who were being held hostage in Iran and by Carter's

The Republican presidential contenders waving to the crowd at Central High School in Manchester, New Hampshire, before a debate, February 20, 1980. Left to right, they are Philip Crane, John Connally, John Anderson, Howard Baker, Robert Dole, Ronald Reagan, and George H. W. Bush

unsuccessful efforts to free them, including an aborted military rescue that cost the lives of eight American servicemen.

Reagan preached optimism. If he were elected, America would stand tall again, he said, and competence would return to Washington.

"Are you better off now than you were four years ago?" he asked voters.

Absolutely not, they responded, and gave him a resounding victory: 51 percent of the vote to Carter's 41 percent. Independent John Anderson won nearly 7 percent.

Reagan won the electoral vote 489 to 44.

Making a point. Candidate Reagan visits the South Bronx in New York City, August 5, 1980, after addressing the National Urban League conference.

Tumultuous First Term

When Reagan took office at the age of sixty-nine, he was better positioned than any Republican since Eisenhower to lay a firm hand on government. He froze hiring and new regulations. He swept even low-level Democrats out of their jobs and replaced them with Republicans. He won a 25 percent cut in personal income taxes and big tax breaks for businesses. He called for deep cuts in social programs, and he increased Pentagon spending by more than 9 percent per year between fiscal 1981 and 1984.

To presidents with programs, their first hundred days in office are important. Reagan did not have that long. On his seventieth day, he was shot by John W. Hinckley Jr., a twenty-five-year-old drifter who had hidden in a crowd of reporters outside the Washington Hilton, where Reagan had just spoken to labor leaders. A .22-caliber bullet entered his chest under his left shoulder. It careened off a rib and lodged in his left lung—within an inch of his heart. The bullet was removed during a two-hour operation, but not before he had lost nearly half his blood and edged close to death.

Reagan had been in far graver danger than he let on. He had walked into the hospital and did not collapse until he was out of sight. "Honey, I forgot to duck," he told Nancy, borrowing a line from boxer Jack Dempsey.

Hinckley, who had a history of psychiatric problems, was trying to impress actress Jodie Foster, whom he idolized. He had fired six shots, wounding four people. Press Secretary James Brady was hit in the head and has been in a wheelchair since. Hinckley was committed to a mental institution.

Twelve days after the shooting, Reagan was back at the White House. His strength and gallant demeanor touched the public. Characteristically, however, he did not change his long-standing opposition to gun control. Brady, on the other hand, became a national leader in the fight to curb handguns.

Despite the interruption, Reagan lost little momentum. In the middle of his first summer as president, more than 11,000 federal air traffic controllers, members of one of the few unions to support him, walked off their jobs—and he fired them. It was a blow to organized labor, already in decline. But it showed that Reagan meant what he said, especially about guarding the economy against inflation. Before the end of his first summer as president, Congress had enacted his historic tax cut and his budget legislation largely intact.

Three images show President Reagan being helped into a limousine after being hit by a bullet fired by John Hinckley outside the Washington Hilton hotel, Monday, March 30, 1981.

In his effort to impress actress Jodie Foster, John Hinckley fired six shots trying to kill President Reagan. Hinckley wounded four men: President Reagan; the president's press secretary James Brady and police officer Tom Delahanty, who are lying on the ground in this picture; and secret service agent Tim McCarthy.

To justify increasing defense spending while slashing taxes, Reagan had embraced supply-side economics—a theory that enjoyed little standing among many economists. Supply-siders held that higher spending and lower taxes would not increase the deficit. Instead, the theory held, tax cuts would unleash such a wave of economic growth that government income would actually rise.

It did not happen. As defense spending rose and the tax cuts kicked in, the predicted surge in economic growth did not materialize. The deficit soared toward record levels. Eventually, the national debt nearly tripled. Before Reagan's first year was up, the nation's economy plunged into the worst downturn in years. By March of 1982, Reagan, who had acknowledged "a slight and, I hope, a short recession," was reduced to denying that the nation was in a depression. Unemployment reached a forty-one-year record of 10.8 percent that November, and the global effects of the slowdown did severe damage to Third World debtor nations and the world's banking system.

Reagan's budget director, David Stockman, was among the disillusioned. He granted a series of devastating interviews to William Greider, who published them in *The Atlantic Monthly*, quoting Stockman as saying, "None of us really understands what's going on with all these numbers."

"Stay the course!" Reagan urged the nation, insisting that supply side simply needed more time. But even Republicans feared that without additional revenue, the deficit would reach uncontrollable proportions. Republican senators forced him to accept a three-year, $100 billion tax increase.

Reagan sought to pass it off as closing loopholes.

The economic turmoil cost the Republicans twenty-five seats in the House of Representatives. But Democrats were hesitant to press their own solutions for the recession, and when Reagan's tax increase began boosting economic indicators in the fall of 1983, the president could claim full credit.

All the while, superpower relations degenerated to an unnerving low. Arms control negotiations stalled. Some Americans, including a number of religious leaders, urged a freeze on nuclear weapons. To blunt the movement, Reagan assailed the Soviet Union as an "evil empire." He called communism "another sad, bizarre chapter in human history whose last pages even now are being written." He announced a plan to develop a space-based defense

system, called the Strategic Defense Initiative (SDI), to destroy Soviet missiles before they could reach the United States.

President Reagan signing the 1981 tax cut bill at his retreat Rancho del Cielo outside Santa Barbara.

Moscow bristled.

American critics said SDI would never work. They named the system Star Wars, after the George Lucas space fantasy film. But Reagan would not give it up, and it became a persistent stumbling block to an arms control agreement.

In September of 1983, a Soviet fighter shot down an unarmed South Korean airliner that had strayed into Soviet air space over a Russian peninsula. The attack killed 269 people, including a U.S. congressman. Although an isolated incident, it deepened fear of a superpower conflict.

In the Middle East, the administration tried hard to bring peace. Reagan sent Marines into Lebanon as part of a multinational force to end warfare between Christians and Muslims. But the administration was divided. Reagan's advisors showed signs of the infighting that would come to cost him dearly during his second term. Defense Secretary Caspar W. Weinberger opposed the mis-

sion in Lebanon. But Reagan, encouraged by Secretary of State George P. Shultz, stepped up U.S. involvement.

Pro-Iranian terrorists crashed a bomb-laden van into the U.S. embassy in Beirut, killing sixty-three people, including seventeen Americans. Reagan held the Marines in place despite the increasing risk.

Terrorists struck again. A truck filled with explosives broke through inadequate defenses around a Marine barracks in Beirut. It blew the building to pieces and killed 241 U.S. servicemen.

It was "the saddest day of my presidency," Reagan wrote in *An American Life*, and "perhaps the saddest day of my life."

On the day after the bombing, he ordered Marines and Army Rangers to invade the Caribbean island of Grenada to oust a cadre of Cuban troops, effectively overthrow a new Marxist government, and bring home eight hundred American medical students. Many allies and a number of Democratic leaders called the invasion meddling in Grenada's affairs and suspected that it was intended to distract Americans from the horror in Beirut.

The facts show otherwise, Cannon said. Although Reagan did not issue his formal order for the invasion until the day after Beirut, planning for a military evacuation of the students from Grenada had been under way for four days, and Reagan and his advisors had reached a consensus to invade the island one day before.

In the end, the 5,000-member invasion force, facing little opposition, sustained nineteen fatalities. But Americans reveled in the show of military muscle.

During all of this, Reagan refused to bring the Marines home from Lebanon. He left them at risk for three more months until he quietly ordered all 1,500 to retreat to the safety of U.S. Navy ships offshore.

By now the economy was back up. The president and the Federal Reserve had curbed inflation, "the most enduring," Cannon judged, "of Reagan's economic legacies."

The president, who might have been doomed by recession and plagued by misadventures abroad, basked in respect. As the 1984 election approached, he held a big lead in the polls.

His television commercials declared: "It's morning again in America."

TRIUMPH AND SCANDAL

Reagan campaigned on patriotism, prosperity and military strength. His opponent, Walter F. Mondale, who was Carter's vice president, failed to seize on a compelling issue. He saddled himself with a pledge to raise taxes. He said Reagan would raise taxes too, but would not be candid enough to admit it ahead of time.

A poor performance during one debate gave Reagan his only uneasy moment. It prompted speculation that the president, well past seventy-three, might be too old for the job. When the matter came up in the next debate, he remarked with a disarming smile, "I want you to know that . . . I will not make age an issue of this campaign. I am not going to exploit, for political purposes, my opponent's youth and inexperience."

Even Mondale, fifty-six, laughed.

Reagan won by the largest electoral raw-vote landslide in history. He received 59 percent of the popular vote, carried 49 states and got 525 electoral votes—to Mondale's 13.

Even before his second inauguration, planning was under way for Reagan to visit Germany for the 1985 economic summit on the fortieth anniversary of the defeat of the Nazis. Chancellor Helmut Kohl asked him to honor dead German soldiers as an act of reconciliation. Touched by Kohl's emotion and eager to reciprocate his support as an ally, Reagan agreed—and kept his word, despite relentless objections from Elie Wiesel and other Jewish leaders, as well as groups of American veterans, prominent Republicans and his own wife, Nancy.

The ceremony would be at a cemetery in Bitburg. Protests exploded into outcries when snow melted on the graves and revealed that 49 SS troops were among the 2,000 German soldiers buried there. Wiesel begged Reagan to abandon the Bitburg visit, citing SS participation in the Holocaust. "One million Jewish children perished," he pleaded. "If I spent my entire life reciting their names, I would die before finishing the task. Mr. President, I have seen children—I have seen them being thrown in the flames alive. Words, they die on my lips. . . . May I, Mr. President, if it's possible at all, implore you to do something else . . . to find another way, another site. That place, Mr. President, is not your place. Your place is with the victims of the SS."

Reagan added a stop to honor the Jews who had died at the Bergen-Belsen concentration camp, but it hardly helped. When the president finally visited the German graves, he lost a measure of his stature in the Jewish community.

"Within two months of Bitburg," Cannon said, "Reagan would authorize the first stages of a backdoor deal with Iran that would demonstrate in even greater measure . . . [his] inadequate historical understanding, political naïveté and awesome presidential stubbornness." Emboldened by his landslide reelection, the Reagan administration reached beyond what was legal and provided arms to the Iranians in return for American hostages in Lebanon—and used proceeds to finance a war by guerrillas, called contras, trying to overthrow the Marxist government of Nicaragua.

The deal developed into a scandal called Iran-contra, and it cost the president mightily.

Nicaragua's governing coalition, the Sandinistas, supported guerrillas of its own, who were trying to overthrow pro-American leaders in El Salvador. The Sandinistas, Reagan told *The Washington Post*, were "terrorists" in a "revolution being exported to the Americas."

As early as 1981, Reagan had approved a request by William J. Casey, his CIA director and a longtime cold warrior, for $19 million to help the contras overthrow the Sandinista government in the name of democracy and anticommunism. It was secret money, and it went to five hundred insurrectionists—including national guard members in the former regime of despised Nicaraguan dictator Anastasio Somoza. Reagan called them "freedom fighters" and "the moral equal of our Founding Fathers."

Rightists won control of the Salvadoran assembly, and they elected as president Roberto d'Aubuisson, suspected of being tied to the unsolved murder of Oscar Arnulfo Romero, a Catholic archbishop and outspoken foe of the far right. Now Reagan found himself supplying covert aid to members of a deposed despot's national guard who were trying to overthrow the lawful government of Nicaragua in defense of a right-wing leader in El Salvador who was associated with death squads.

Reagan did not flinch. In 1982, *The Washington Post* disclosed his covert aid. He won several fights in Congress to send the contras official assistance, but he lost others, and by May of 1984 the contras were broke. Robert C. McFarlane, the president's national security advisor, said Reagan told him to keep the contras together "body and soul."

McFarlane passed the instruction along to a Marine lieutenant colonel, Oliver North, who was a member of the National Security Council staff.

Congress passed an amendment, called Boland II, barring the use of funds to support, either directly or indirectly, any military or paramilitary operations in Nicaragua. Less than a month before his reelection, Reagan signed the legislation. But he thought that helping the contras was the "right thing to do," according to Cannon. "He had no interest whatever in the legal restrictions that Congress believed it had imposed on him."

At the same time, his second term brought an acute deterioration in his White House team, with disastrous consequences. He allowed James A. Baker, his pragmatic chief of staff, to trade jobs with Donald Regan, his secretary of the Treasury. For four years, said Jane Mayer and Doyle McManus, Baker had helped guard Reagan "from his own worst instincts." Regan, on the other hand, let Reagan be Reagan. The loss of Baker at the White House, along with his political savvy, was widely blamed for many of the subsequent troubles that befell the president.

Regan and McFarlane distrusted each other; Cannon said they barely spoke. McFarlane also was at odds with Secretary of State Shultz and Secretary of Defense Weinberger, especially on Iran. McFarlane wanted to woo Iran away from Soviet influence, even if it meant encouraging the sale of Western arms to Iran for its ongoing war against Iraq. Shultz and Weinberger opposed it adamantly. American policy forbade selling arms to Iran and other sponsors of terrorism.

To Reagan, this was yet another wrangle over government policy. He was not really interested in government, Cannon said. He "was so obviously wearied by extensive analysis, particularly of foreign policy, that aides plunged into arcane material at their peril. If Reagan became sufficiently bored, he simply nodded off."

He had even less appetite for personal conflicts among his staff. "Reagan had learned in childhood from his father's alcoholic eruptions to withdraw at any sign of disharmony," Cannon said.

In March of 1984, William Buckley, the CIA station chief in Beirut, had been kidnapped by terrorists linked to Iran, and CIA director Casey told Reagan he wanted Buckley back. Moreover, Casey saw merit in McFarlane's cold war view of Iran as a barrier against the Soviet Union.

Terrorists took more hostages, seven Americans in all.

This seized Reagan's attention like no policy debate ever could. It evoked what Mayer and McManus call the "hard-liner's soft touch." The danger, they say, "was that, left to his own good intentions, the president would confuse the human interest with the national interest. . . . There was no clearer example of this danger than in his approach to the hostages."

In August of 1985, McFarlane later testified, Reagan secretly approved the first of eight shipments of missiles and missile parts to Iran. Four of the shipments were made through Israel, which provided the arms and received replacements from the United States. The other shipments were made directly.

Reagan signed three "findings," or authorizations, for the secret sales. One spoke of freeing the hostages. Attached to another was a memo. Cannon says Reagan did not bother to read it, so Admiral John Poindexter, who had succeeded McFarlane as national security advisor, initialed it on Reagan's behalf. It approved using a private agent as a go-between.

North already had arranged for such an agent. He called it the Enterprise. It was a network of secret operatives, shadow corporations and Swiss bank accounts. He could use them to do something that might be illegal under Boland II but would further a cause dear to the president. He could divert profits from the Iranian arms sales to the contras. It would keep them together "body and soul."

Secretly, Cannon says, North and the Enterprise demanded far more money from the Iranians than they paid the Defense Department for the missiles; just two of the shipments had yielded $6.3 million in profits. North kept none of the money for himself, but fellow operatives in the Enterprise pocketed some. North gave much of the rest to the Contras.

On November 3, 1986, a Lebanese magazine, *Al-Shiraa*, told about a McFarlane visit to Iran and said he had sent weapons on Reagan's behalf. Three days later the *Los Angeles Times* and *The Washington Post* broke the first full story of the Iran arms sales. Diversion of profits to the contras remained a secret, but Congress exploded in anger, and the trading of arms for hostages sputtered to a close.

By Cannon's count, Reagan had sold more than 2,000 missiles and in excess of 200 spare parts to Iran. Operatives in the Enterprise had pocketed $4.4 million. Another $3.8 million had gone to the contras, in defiance of the law established by Boland II. The CIA's Buckley had died in captivity. Three American hostages had been released, but terrorists had taken three others in their stead.

The president's first reaction was a "no comment," his second, a denial. Then his denial became confusing: He said that Weinberger and Shultz had supported an initiative toward Iran, which he had already denied existed. He refused to concede that he had traded arms for hostages. "Our government has a firm policy not to capitulate to terrorist demands," he declared to the American people in a televised speech. "That no-concessions policy remains in force, in spite of the wildly speculative and false stories about arms for hostages and alleged ransom payments.

"We did not—repeat, did not—trade weapons or anything else for hostages."

This became his version of the truth, Cannon said, and the one that Reagan believed forever. A *Los Angeles Times* poll found, however, that only 14 percent of those who watched him on television believed him.

Attorney General Edwin Meese III opened an inquiry. So did congressional committees and a bipartisan review board headed by former Senator John G. Tower, a Republican from Texas. An independent counsel, former federal judge Lawrence Walsh, a Republican, began a criminal investigation.

Meese's investigation discovered the diversion of funds to the contras. Now the attorney general and other top aides worried that the president might be impeached. McFarlane tried to kill himself. Reagan forced Poindexter to resign. He fired North, then called him "a national hero." The

Tower commission said that Regan, as chief of staff, bore "primary responsibility for the chaos that had descended upon the White House." Reagan forced Regan to resign.

Attorney General Edwin Meese moves to the podium to answer reporters' questions on Iran-contra in the White House Briefing Room, November 25, 1986. Proceeds from the secret sale of arms to Iran had been diverted to the U.S.-backed contras fighting the government in Nicaragua.

Walsh indicted fourteen people, mostly lesser players. They included Poindexter, who was convicted of five felony counts of conspiracy, obstruction of Congress and lying to Congress. His conviction was overturned. Walsh charged Weinberger with perjury. But before Weinberger could be tried, he was pardoned by Reagan's vice president, George H. W. Bush, after he was elected president.

Ten others were convicted. Walsh found that Reagan had "participated or acquiesced in covering up the scandal."

Had he authorized sending money from Iran to the contras? Walsh could not find out.

Reagan consistently denied it.

The answer was a mystery and might be forever.

In 1985, Reagan underwent surgery for colon cancer. A recuperating president, accompanied by the first lady, waves from the window of the president's room at the National Naval Medical Center in Bethesda, Maryland, July 1985.

A THAW IN COLD WAR

In domestic policy, Reagan came under attack for responding too slowly to the growing health threat of AIDS, but he won praise, at least from conservatives, for keeping his pledge to change the Supreme Court.

In 1981, he appointed the first woman, Sandra Day O'Connor, a moderately conservative judge from Arizona. In 1986, he promoted conservative Justice William H. Rehnquist to be chief justice and appointed another conservative, Antonin Scalia.

He nominated Robert H. Bork, the conservative who fired special prosecutor Archibald Cox for Richard Nixon during Watergate. But the nomination was defeated after a battle that injected enduring bitterness into confirmation hearings. Reagan had to settle for Anthony M. Kennedy. While hardly a liberal, Kennedy later would vote against overturning *Roe v. Wade*, which upholds the right to abortion.

Nor was Iran-contra the only trouble abroad. In late 1985, four Palestinians hijacked the Italian cruise ship *Achille Lauro* with four hundred passengers aboard. The hijackers surrendered in Egypt, but not before killing Leon Klinghoffer, sixty-nine, a New Yorker confined to a wheelchair. He was singled out because he was Jewish.

When an Egyptian plane tried to fly the hijackers home, U.S. Navy fighters forced it to land in Sicily, where they were arrested. The interception gave the administration a boost.

In April 1986, American planes struck Libya in retaliation for a terrorist attack on a West Berlin nightclub that claimed the life of a U.S. serviceman. Libyan officials said leader Moammar Kadafi was not harmed, but three dozen civilians were killed, including his adopted daughter, and that nearly a hundred people, including two of his sons, were injured.

The raid was sharply criticized internationally, but it, too, gained Reagan popularity at home.

His overwhelming triumph, however, was an improvement in superpower relations that presaged the end of the cold war. Nothing displayed Reagan's capacity for political accommodation more clearly than his dealings with Soviet leader Mikhail S. Gorbachev.

During his second term, Reagan carried the burden of his anti-Soviet rhetoric and the stakes he had raised with SDI, his space-based defense program, into four summit meetings with Gorbachev. Reagan doggedly pursued both a reduction in nuclear weapons and better treatment for dissidents and Soviet Jews.

Reagan had three good reasons to reach out to Gorbachev, Cannon says. He had little to show for his first four years in foreign policy. He had built up the military and could bargain from strength. He was freer to deal with the Soviets than any other president because he, of all people, could not be accused of being soft on communism.

Reagan believed in Armageddon. It made him a visionary. "My dream . . . became a world free of nuclear weapons," he said in *An American Life*. Because "I knew it would be a long and difficult task to rid the world of nuclear weapons, I had this second dream: the creation of a defense against nuclear missiles, so we could change from a policy of assured destruction to one of assured survival."

But during negotiations, Cannon said, his two dreams clashed. The Soviets refused to retire any of their strategic long-range missiles unless Reagan gave up SDI, his proposed system of defensive missiles to knock down enemy weapons. SDI frightened the Soviets. If it ever worked, they said, it would provide a screen behind which the United States could launch an atomic attack of its own.

Moreover, they said, SDI violated an antiballistic missile treaty in effect since 1972. The treaty permitted laboratory research of antimissile components, but it banned testing and deployment.

On this, too, the Reagan administration was divided. Defense Secretary Weinberger and Assistant Defense Secretary Richard Perle wanted a broader interpretation of the treaty to permit testing. Secretary of State Shultz and Paul Nitze, his leading arms negotiator, said anything but the traditional interpretation would anger the Soviets and cause problems with allies and members of Congress.

As usual, Cannon says, Reagan tried to avoid the disagreement. He said he would interpret the ABM treaty broadly to permit testing, but as a matter of policy he would abide by the traditional interpretation and stop short of conducting any tests.

"A deliberate deceit," the Soviets responded.

So it was that prospects seemed dim when Reagan and Gorbachev sat down on November 19, 1985, in Geneva for their first summit. Reagan was the first U.S. president since Eisenhower to go more than four years without meeting his Soviet counterpart. During those four years, there were three Soviet leaders. They "kept dying on me," he quipped.

From the start, Reagan was relaxed and cordial. As Gorbachev, bundled against the cold, approached the mansion on Lake Geneva where they would hold their initial session, Reagan took off his overcoat and strode out onto the top step to greet him.

In *An American Life*, he wrote: "As we shook hands for the first time, I had to admit—as Margaret Thatcher and [Canadian] Prime Minister Brian Mulroney predicted I would—that there was something likable about Gorbachev."

During their first meeting, Reagan has a fireside chat with his Soviet counterpart, Mikhail Gorbachev, at the Hotel Fleur D'Eau in Geneva, November 19, 1985.

Reagan developed a personal sense of Gorbachev as someone he could deal with. But by afternoon the two of them were arguing about SDI. Reagan said the United States would never launch an initial strike with nuclear weapons and would prove it by sharing SDI technology with the Soviets.

Gorbachev did not believe him. For his part, the Soviet leader said that his nation had no aggressive intentions.

How could Americans believe that, Reagan asked, if Gorbachev did not believe him?

Reagan suggested some fresh air. He and Gorbachev strolled out to a pool house and talked in front of a blazing fire. They achieved no momentous breakthrough, but as they walked back, Reagan invited Gorbachev to meet again, this time in Washington. Gorbachev accepted and proposed a subsequent meeting in Moscow.

It set the stage for negotiation, not denunciation. The two leaders shared "a kind of chemistry," Reagan told Cannon. "Yes, we argued, and we'd go nose to nose. But when the argument was over, it was like it is with us. He wasn't stalking out of there and [saying] 'down with the lousy Americans' or anything. We fought it out, and maybe knew we were going to fight it out again, but when the meeting was over, we were normal."

In *An American Life*, Reagan said he was reminded of his after-hours relationship with Tip O'Neill. The Soviet leader "could tell jokes about himself and even about his country, and I grew to like him more."

They ended the summit with a promise: to seek a 50 percent cut in nuclear weapons.

It looked impossible. Gorbachev remained adamant: no SDI, or no cuts. Reagan was committed to both: SDI and cuts. Worse, Cannon says, Reagan's advisors were more sharply divided than ever. Weinberger and Perle distrusted arms control and wanted SDI, at least partly to block an agreement. But Shultz and Nitze wanted an agreement so badly they were willing to give ground on SDI.

Gorbachev suggested meeting in Iceland or Britain before the Washington summit to see if he and Reagan could break the deadlock. Reagan chose Iceland. They met on October 11, 1986, in Reykjavik. The two leaders argued about the missile cuts and about SDI, and their advisors negotiated through the night. By morning, they had neared agreement on the cuts—but they remained far apart on SDI.

In *An American Life*, Reagan says that Gorbachev would not budge on any SDI development outside the laboratory.

Reagan stood. "The meeting is over." He turned to Shultz. "Let's go, George. We're leaving."

Shultz was crushed, but Reagan was unfazed. "I went to Reykjavik determined that everything was negotiable except two things," he told the American people afterward. "Our freedom and our future."

Over the coming year, Shultz, Gorbachev and his advisors negotiated persistently to eliminate at least a lower level of weaponry: the U.S. and Soviet arsenals of intermediate- and short-range missiles. In September 1987, Shultz and Soviet foreign minister Eduard Shevardnadze announced an agreement in principle on an Intermediate Nuclear Forces treaty, and Gorbachev came to Washington that December.

General Secretary Gorbachev and President Reagan looking tense after a meeting in Reykjavík, October 1986. In Iceland, Gorbachev proposed to Reagan that he curtail development of the Star Wars program.

INITIATIVE

SDI

To mark the fifth anniversary of his Strategic Defense Initiative, or Star Wars, the president addresses a conference in Washington, D.C., in March 1988. With him are physicist Dr. Edward Teller, the father of the hydrogen bomb, and SDI director Lieutenant General James A. Abrahamson.

Dr. Edward Teller

President
RONALD REAGAN

Crowds along the streets applauded him. Like an American politician, Gorbachev stopped his car, got out and shook hands.

On December 8, Reagan and the Soviet leader sat at a White House table once used by Abraham Lincoln and put their names to a ban on all nuclear missiles with ranges of 300 miles to 3,400 miles.

The destruction of these missiles—about 1,700 by the Soviet Union and 800 by the United States—was well under way by the time Reagan left office.

As for the long-range missiles, it was obvious before the remaining Reagan-Gorbachev summit in Moscow that SDI would be an insurmountable obstacle to any reduction. But Reagan went to the Soviet Union anyway.

He received a welcome from the Russians to match Gorbachev's in America. As Reagan walked through the Arbat, where artisans sold their wares, crowds pressed forward to greet him. KGB agents charged the people, causing a panic. But their friendly intentions carried the day.

Reagan spoke to students at Moscow State University, offering them his vision of the American dream. He met with ninety-six dissidents and pressed Gorbachev on human rights.

Gorbachev already had allowed hundreds to emigrate who were on lists Reagan had given him, and he would free thousands more.

Reagan met three more times with Gorbachev. Once was in New York when the Soviet leader spoke to the United Nations; the second time was in San Francisco, after Reagan had left office; and the third time was in Moscow, when Reagan was nearly two years into retirement.

By now, Reagan was calling Gorbachev "my friend."

Reagan never abandoned what he said was his favorite Russian proverb, *doveryai no proveryai*, "trust but verify." But the warmth of their friendship started the thaw that ended the cold war.

GOING HOME HAPPY

When he departed the White House and came back to California, Ronald Reagan had good reason to be satisfied. He had failed to balance the federal budget; the national debt had nearly tripled to $2.68 trillion. But his recession, which Cannon calls "the worst since the Depression," had been followed by what would become the longest peacetime recovery in history.

Reagan had achieved an unprecedented breakthrough in arms control, and his diplomacy had been crucial to peace. He was, Gorbachev declared, a "great political leader."

His credibility with Congress and the American people, dismayingly low during Iran-contra, had recovered. His achievements as well as his unyielding belief that nothing was impossible and his uncanny ability to persuade Americans to believe in him and in themselves had earned Ronald Reagan a job performance rating in the Gallup poll of 63 percent when he left Washington. It had been 51 percent when he arrived.

On January 11, 1989, when he bade farewell from the Oval Office, there were two things he was proudest of. "One is the economic recovery. . . . The other is the recovery of our morale. America is respected again in the world, and looked to for leadership."

The United States, he said, was a shining city upon a hill. "And how stands the city on this winter night? More prosperous, more secure and happier than it was eight years ago. But more than that. After two hundred years, two centuries, she still stands strong and true on the granite ridge, and her glow has held steadily no matter what the storm. . . .

"As I walk off into the city streets, a final word to the men and women across America, who for eight years did the work that brought America back: My friends, we did it. We weren't just marking time, we made a difference. We made the city stronger, we made the city freer, and we left her in good hands.

"All in all, not bad. Not bad at all. And so, goodbye. God bless you. And God bless the United States of America."

Times *staff writers Richard T. Cooper in Washington and Carl Ingram in Sacramento and researchers Anna M. Virtue in Miami and Jacquelyn Cenacveira and Janet Lundblad in Los Angeles contributed to this story.*

After leaving the White House for the last time as president, Reagan waves good-bye from the door of Air Force One at Andrews Air Force Base as he and Nancy prepare to return home to California, January 20, 1989.

PART TWO

THE GREAT COMMUNICATOR

THE GREAT COMMUNICATOR

by Lesley Stahl

When I was the CBS correspondent covering the Jimmy Carter White House, my daughter, then eight, would tell people: "The president works for my mommy." When Ronald Reagan came into office she turned it around: "Mommy works for the president." Even a little girl could feel the force of the Great Communicator. Without once raising his voice, Ronald Reagan sold the country on his dreams and illusions, and he sold himself as a strong leader.

There was some secret alchemy when he spoke to the nation, with those sunny eyes and voice soft as cashmere. Time and again in his presidency, the CBS News/*New York Times* polls showed that even people who disagreed with his policies nonetheless trusted him at the helm and wanted him to remain there.

The trusting started early on when he was shot by John Hinckley and joked about it (at the hospital to Nancy: "Honey, I forgot to duck!"). He was seen as heroic and gritty, an image solidified five months later when he took on the air traffic controllers, which, of course, he did on television: "They're in violation of the law," he said about their strike. And he fired them. He was like the sheriff in the Old West, come to clean up the town.

One of his close aides told me: "He may have been the most passive man I ever met in public life." But somehow he was convincing as an activist cowboy (which he wasn't), a family man (he was divorced and rarely saw his children), and a war hero (he never went to battle).

Being an actor was part of his secret. No president was ever that at ease before the cameras, and cowboys are always at ease. He came across on television as natural, easy in his laugh and his walk.

A big part of the secret was his disposition. Temperament is destiny. I always felt that his greatest strength was his innate sweetness. When Ronald Reagan was "communicating," he oozed sunniness. At one point when the deficit was ballooning, he went on what you might call a cheerful rampage against those who criticized Reaganomics. Republican leaders were "sob sisters": as phrases go, not exactly a weapon of mass destruction. The Democrats were "born-again budget balancers"—more alliterative than acerbic. There was almost always the light touch. And when he went too far, he'd pull back. The press corps: we were "the messengers of gloom and doom." But when he charged that our negative reporting was prolonging the recession, he apologized. "Presidents, even Thomas Jefferson," he said, "have their moods just like everyone else."

I can tell you firsthand that his "likability" was a mighty force. It was a package—of geniality, politeness, open smiles—that was irresistible. There was hardly anyone he couldn't disarm. One cold day in February 1981 members of the Congressional Black Caucus stormed up the White House driveway, telling us reporters they were there to give the president a piece of their minds over his plans to cut poverty programs like school lunches (ketchup was a vegetable). But after the meeting, they were puppy dogs. I reported, "They were lullabyed." I saw that happen over and over.

So he was nice, but at the same time tough as John Wayne when it came to his core issues. Not even his wife could budge him from one of his deeply felt convictions. Presidential historian Richard Reeves called it Reagan's "stubborn integrity" when he'd stay with an issue, even in the face of widespread criticism.

The CBS pollster Kathy Frankovic told me that much of Reagan's popularity derived from his aura of consistency. This was something he worked at communicating. Even when he didn't stick to his guns, he *said* he did! Reagan *raised* taxes over and over, but each time he would insist he was a tax cutter, and persuaded everyone he was. Now, that's communicating.

His sense of humor was also key. He was genuinely witty, and realized that being funny, especially about himself, was central to his popularity. He often made fun of his age (my favorite: "I did turn seventy-five today, but remember, that's only twenty-four Celsius!"); of his lazy work habits ("They say hard work never hurt anybody, but I figure: why take the chance!"); of his conservative team ("Sometimes our right hand doesn't know what our far-right hand is doing!"). And no one could deliver the jokes better.

Or deliver a speech better. On a trip to his presidential library in Simi

Valley, California, I got to look through his speech files and was astonished to see how deeply he had been immersed in the writing. I had such a fixed notion of Reagan as a floater over the events of his presidency—even the decision making—that I was startled by his handwritten revisions on page after page. He invariably simplified the draft language and infused energy and color.

He wrote most of the speech he gave after the bombing of the U.S. military barracks in Lebanon. "This past Sunday at twenty-two minutes after six Beirut time, with dawn just breaking . . ." He wrote a scene that was cinematic: "At the wheel was a young man on a suicide mission." Most presidents lecture or give you a laundry list. Reagan created an adventure about brave American kids standing up to the big bad Commies. He wasn't just an actor who read his lines well; he

wrote them, and sold us his pretty illusions. Lou Cannon, Reagan's biographer, wrote that he made sense of the world narratively, through stories, which are not always logical.

Last-minute polish. From his private White House study, Reagan studies the text of his second inaugural address, January 18, 1985.

Nor, as it turned out, always accurate. Reagan loved to tell anecdotes, again with visual immediacy, as a way to hold his audience's attention, and reinforce a point. But often the facts in his anecdotes didn't hold up. Typical was a story he told about cutting social programs, like the hot meals for the elderly in Pima County, Arizona. Of the $53,000 budget, he said, "Fifty thousand dollars went for staffing and administration overhead." When "they eliminated the overhead," he said, "and ran the program with volunteers . . . they saved $47,000 and ended up feeding twice as many people." Only trouble, it wasn't true.

To illustrate what's wrong with food stamps, in 1982 he told an audience about a young man in a grocery store who bought an orange with his food stamps and "took the change and paid for [a bottle of] vodka." The only trouble with that was, change from food stamps was limited to ninety-nine cents.

He also mangled quotes and facts. The press would report the inaccuracies as gaffes and goofs, but the public didn't seem to mind, and considered the misstatements all but irrelevant.

Even with his acting and writing skills, and his personal drive, Reagan might not have accomplished as much as he did if he hadn't hired Mike Deaver as his media guru. Here was a man who understood television better than those of us who worked in television.

Deaver created little movies starring Rawhide (Reagan's Secret Service code name). He chopped wood to tell us visually: See, I'm *not* old. Nancy and he walked arm-in-arm: We *are* a close family.

Just before the 1984 election, I put together a report for the evening news about the reelection campaign. My point was these Deaver "photo ops" were an attempt to create amnesia about Reagan's weak spots.

My report said: To deal with the criticism that he was "the rich man's president, you saw pictures of him picnicking with ordinary folks, surrounded by black kids . . . or farmers." To obscure that he had tried to cut the budget for the handicapped and housing for the elderly, you saw him at the Special Olympics and the opening of a nursing home.

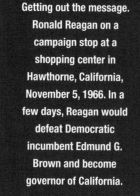

Getting out the message. Ronald Reagan on a campaign stop at a shopping center in Hawthorne, California, November 5, 1966. In a few days, Reagan would defeat Democratic incumbent Edmund G. Brown and become governor of California.

I thought: This is so tough, no one at the White House will ever talk to me again. But I was wrong. They loved the piece, even thanked me, explaining that all the public noticed were the pictures of a hale and caring Reagan. "When the pictures are dramatic," a White House official explained, "they overcome the sound. Lesley, nobody *heard* what you said." I was being told something we in TV-land hadn't figured out. When the Reagan White House would say "We have to feed the beast," they meant feed the press these pretty visuals with the hidden messages. We lapped them up not like "the beast" but like hungry puppies, and so did the public.

One of Deaver's masterpieces was the memorial service in December 1985 after a plane carrying troops home from duty

in the Middle East crashed in Newfoundland. All aboard were killed. Five days later at Fort Campbell, Kentucky, the Reagans embraced each and every one of the 350 mourners. Nancy held sobbing wives, touched a picture of a son; the president hugged a black man.

How warm, how compassionate. That's what the pictures conveyed. And yet Reagan was trying to cut social programs, seemingly oblivious of the needs of the poor. How could anyone that kind be so unconcerned about poverty?

His biographer, Edmund Morris, a great admirer of the president, told me in an interview for *60 Minutes* that he was disturbed by a coldness he detected. "He wasn't compassionate. . . . I think Reagan regarded misfortune as a weakness. There was something undignified about poverty. . . . He didn't like it; he didn't want to see it."

But Ronald Reagan accomplished big things by pursuing a grand vision relentlessly. With a focused determination, he altered the American conversation; he changed our goals. And even as he bashed the government and sought to dismantle it, he demonstrated that it could work.

In his time there was more greed, more sex and violence in our media, more AIDS, more single-parent families, and more divorce. And yet he persuaded much of the country that we lived in "a shining city on a hill." It was an illusion, but one that was good for the soul.

When I asked Edmund Morris if he thought Reagan was one of our best presidents, he said, "I think he stands way up there. I think he was a great man and a great president."

"Are you talking about the fall of communism?" I asked.

"Yes, and the moral regeneration of the United States. When he became president, we were full of self-doubts. The national spirit was at rock bottom and overnight there was this mysterious change in the national self-image. It was so quick it can only be ascribed to him."

But not even Morris could explain how Reagan had done it. Surely it was part optimism, part salesmanship, part a gift for language, but it was also something more. Trying to explain why America loved Reagan is ultimately as hopeless as trying to define why you love whomever you love. Tell me how love works and I'll tell you how the Great Communicator seduced us.

Selection from Speech for Barry Goldwater, October 27, 1964

Ronald Reagan's national political debut came in the form
of a televised address he made in support of Republican
presidential candidate Barry Goldwater on October 27,
1964. This is part of what came to be known in Reagan
lore simply as "The Speech."

———————

Thank you very much. Thank you and good evening. The sponsor has been identified, but unlike most television programs, the performer hasn't been provided with a script. As a matter of fact, I have been permitted to choose my own ideas regarding the choice that we face in the next few weeks.

I have spent most of my life as a Democrat. I recently have seen fit to follow another course. I believe that the issues confronting us cross party lines. Now, one side in this campaign has been telling us that the issues of this election are the maintenance of peace and prosperity. The line has been used "We've never had it so good."

But I have an uncomfortable feeling that this prosperity isn't something on which we can base our hopes for the future. No nation in history has ever survived a tax burden that reached a third of its national income. Today, 37 cents of every dollar earned in this country is the tax collector's share, and yet our government continues to spend $17 million a day more than the government takes in. We haven't balanced our budget twenty-eight out of the last thirty-four years. We have raised our debt limit three times in the last twelve months, and now our national debt is one and a half times bigger than all the combined debts of all the nations in the world. We have $15 billion in gold in our treasury—we don't own an ounce. Foreign dollar claims are $27.3 billion, and we have just had announced that the dollar of 1939 will now purchase 45 cents in its total value.

As for the peace that we would preserve, I wonder who among us would like to approach the wife or mother whose husband or son has died in South Vietnam and ask them if they think this is a peace that should be maintained indefinitely. Do they mean peace, or do they mean we just want to be left in peace? There can be no real peace while one American is dying someplace in the world for the rest of us. We are at war with the most dangerous enemy that has ever faced mankind in his long climb from the swamp to the stars, and it has been said if we lose that war, and in doing so lose this way of freedom of ours, history will record with the greatest astonishment that those who had the most to lose did the least to prevent its happening. Well, I think it's time we ask ourselves if we still know the freedoms that were intended for us by the Founding Fathers.

Not too long ago two friends of mine were talking to a Cuban refugee, a businessman who had escaped from Castro, and in the midst of his story one of my friends turned to the other and said, "We don't know how lucky we are." And the Cuban stopped and said, "How lucky you are! I had someplace to escape to." In that sentence he told us the entire story. If we lose freedom here, there is no place to escape to. This is the last stand on Earth. And this idea that government is beholden to the people, that it has no other source of power except to sovereign people, is still the newest and most unique idea in all the long history of man's relation to man. This is the issue of this election. Whether we believe in our capacity for self-government or whether we abandon the American revolution and confess that a little intellectual elite in a far-distant capital can plan our lives for us better than we can plan them ourselves.

You and I are told increasingly that we have to choose between a left or right, but I would like to suggest that there is no such thing as a left or right. There is only an up or down—up to a man's age-old dream, the ultimate in individual freedom consistent with law and order—or down to the ant heap totalitarianism, and regardless of their sincerity, their humanitarian motives, those who would trade our freedom for security have embarked on this downward course.

In this vote-harvesting time, they use terms like the "Great Society," or as we were told a few days ago by the president, we must accept a "greater government activity in the affairs of the people." But they have been a little more explicit in the past and among themselves—and all of the things that I now will quote have appeared in print. These are not Republican accusations. For example, they have voices that say "the cold war will end through acceptance of a not undemocratic socialism." Another voice says that the profit motive has become outmoded, it must be replaced by the incentives of the welfare state; or our traditional system of individual freedom is incapable of solving the complex problems of the twentieth century. Senator Fulbright has said at Stanford University that the Constitution is outmoded. He referred to the president as our moral teacher and our leader, and he said he is hobbled in his task by the restrictions in power imposed on him by this antiquated document. He must be freed so that he can do for us what he knows is best. And Senator Clark of Pennsylvania, another articulate spokesman, defines liberalism as "meeting the material needs of the masses through the full power of centralized government." Well, I for one resent it when a representative of the people refers to you and me—the free man and woman of this country—as "the masses." This is a term we haven't applied to ourselves in America. But beyond that, "the full power of centralized government"—this was the very thing the Founding Fathers sought to minimize. They knew that governments don't control things. A government can't control the economy without controlling people. And they know when a government sets out to do that, it must use force and coercion to achieve its purpose. They also knew, those Founding Fathers, that outside of its legitimate functions, government does nothing as well or as economically as the private sector of the economy . . .

No government ever voluntarily reduces itself in size. Government programs, once launched, never disappear. Actually, a government bureau is the nearest thing to eternal life we'll ever see on this Earth. Federal employees number 2.5 million, and federal, state, and local, one out of six of the nation's workforce is employed by the government. These proliferating bureaus with their thousands of regulations have cost us many of our constitutional safeguards. How many of us realize that today federal agents can invade a man's property without a warrant? They can impose a fine without a formal hearing, let alone a trial by jury, and they can seize and sell his property in auction to enforce the payment of that fine. In Chico County, Arkansas, James Wier overplanted his rice allotment. The government obtained a $17,000 judgment, and a U.S. marshal sold his 950-acre farm at auction. The government said it was necessary as a warning to others to make the system work. Last February 19 at the University of Minnesota, Norman Thomas, six-time candidate for president on the Socialist Party ticket, said, "If Barry Goldwater became president, he would stop the advance of socialism in the United States." I think that's exactly what he will do.

As a former Democrat, I can tell you Norman Thomas isn't the only man who has drawn this parallel to socialism with the present administration. Back in 1936, Mr. Democrat himself, Al Smith, the great American, came before the American people and charged that the leadership of his party was taking the party of Jefferson, Jackson, and Cleveland down the road under the banners of Marx, Lenin, and Stalin. And he walked away from his party, and he never returned to the day he died, because to this day, the leadership of that party has been taking that party, that honorable party, down the road in the image of the labor socialist party of England. Now it doesn't require expropriation or confiscation of private property or business to impose socialism on a people. What does it mean whether you hold the deed or the title to your business or property if the government holds the power of life and death over that business or property? Such machinery already exists. The government can find some charge to bring against any concern it chooses to prosecute. Every businessman has his own tale of harassment. Somewhere a perversion has taken place. Our natural, inalienable rights are now considered to be a dispensation of government, and freedom has never been so fragile, so close to slipping from our grasp as it is at this moment. Our Democratic opponents seem unwilling to debate these issues. They want to make you and me believe that this is a contest between two men . . . that we are to choose just between two personalities.

Well, what of this man that they would destroy? And in destroying, they would destroy that which he represents, the ideas that you and I hold dear. Is he the brash and shallow and trigger-happy man they say he is? Well, I have been privileged to know him when. I knew him long before he ever dreamed of trying for high office, and I can tell you personally I have

66

never known a man in my life I believe so incapable of doing a dishonest or dishonorable thing.

This is a man who in his own business, before he entered politics, instituted a profit-sharing plan, before unions had ever thought of it. He put in health and medical insurance for all his employees. He took 50 percent of the profits before taxes and set up a retirement program, a pension plan for all his employees. He sent checks for life to an employee who was ill and couldn't work. He provided nursing care for the children of mothers who work in the stores. When Mexico was ravaged by floods from the Rio Grande, he climbed in his airplane and flew medicine and supplies down there.

An ex-GI told me how he met him. It was the week before Christmas during the Korean War, and he was at the Los Angeles airport trying to get a ride home to Arizona for Christmas, and he said that there were a lot of servicemen there and no seats available on the planes. Then a voice came over the loudspeaker and said, "Any men in uniform wanting a ride to Arizona, go to runway such-and-such," and they went down there, and there was this fellow named Barry Goldwater sitting in his plane. Every day in the weeks before Christmas, all day long, he would load up the plane, fly to Arizona, fly them to their homes, then fly back over to get another load.

During the hectic split-second timing of a campaign, this is a man who took time out to sit beside an old friend who was dying of cancer. His campaign managers were understandably impatient, but he said, "There aren't many left who care what happens to her. I'd like her to know I care." This is a man who said to his nineteen-year-old son, "There is no foundation like the rock of honesty and fairness, and when you begin to build your life upon that rock, with the cement of the faith in God that you have, then you have a real start." This is not a man who could carelessly send other people's sons to war. And that is the issue of this campaign that makes all of the other problems I have discussed academic, unless we realize that we are in a war that must be won.

Those who would trade our freedom for the soup kitchen of the welfare state have told us that they have a utopian solution of peace without victory. They call their policy "accommodation." And they say if we only avoid any direct confrontation with the enemy, he will forget his evil ways and learn to love us. All who oppose them are indicted as warmongers. They say we offer simple answers to complex problems. Well, perhaps there is a simple answer—not an easy answer, but simple.

If you and I have the courage to tell our elected officials that we want our national policy based upon what we know in our hearts is morally right. We cannot buy our security, our freedom from the threat of the bomb by committing an immorality so great as saying to a billion now in slavery behind the Iron Curtain, "Give up your dreams of freedom because to save our own skin, we are willing to make a deal with your slave masters." Alexander Hamilton said, "A nation which can prefer disgrace to danger is prepared for a master, and deserves one." Let's set the record straight. There is no argument over the choice between peace and war, but there is only one guaranteed way you can have peace and you can have it in the next second—surrender.

Admittedly there is a risk in any course we follow other than this, but every lesson in history tells us that the greater risk lies in appeasement, and this is the specter our well-meaning liberal friends refuse to face—that their policy of accommodation is appeasement, and it gives no choice between peace and war, only between fight and surrender. If we continue to accommodate, continue to back and retreat, eventually we have to face the final demand—the ultimatum. And what then? When Nikita Khrushchev has told his people he knows what our answer will be? He has told them that we are retreating under the pressure of the cold war, and someday when the time comes to deliver the ultimatum, our surrender will be voluntary because by that time we will have weakened from within spiritually, morally, and economically. He believes this because from our side he has heard voices pleading for "peace at any price" or "better Red than dead," or as one commentator put it, he would rather "live on his knees than die on his feet." And therein lies the road to war, because those voices don't speak for the rest of us. You and I know and do not believe that life is so dear and peace so sweet as to be purchased at the price of chains and slavery. If nothing in life is worth dying for, when did this begin—just in the face of this enemy? Or should Moses have told the children of Israel to live in slavery under the pharaohs? Should Christ have refused the cross? Should the patriots at Concord Bridge have thrown down their guns and refused to fire the shot heard 'round the world? The martyrs of history were not fools, and our honored dead who gave their lives to stop the advance of the Nazis didn't die in vain. Where, then, is the road to peace? Well, it's a simple answer after all.

You and I have the courage to say to our enemies, "There is a price we will not pay." There is a point beyond which they must not advance. This is the meaning in the phrase of Barry Goldwater's "peace through strength." Winston Churchill said that "the destiny of man is not measured by material computation. When great forces are on the move in the world, we learn we are spirits—not animals." And he said, "There is something going on in time and space, and beyond time and space, which, whether we like it or not, spells duty."

You and I have a rendezvous with destiny. We will preserve for our children this, the last best hope of man on Earth, or we will sentence them to take the last step into a thousand years of darkness.

We will keep in mind and remember that Barry Goldwater has faith in us. He has faith that you and I have the ability and the dignity and the right to make our own decisions and determine our own destiny.

Thank you very much.

Text of First Inaugural
Address, January 20, 1981

*Having been sworn in as fortieth president of the
United States, Ronald Reagan delivered his first
inaugural address.*

———————

Senator Hatfield, Mr. Chief Justice, Mr. President, Vice President
Bush, Vice President Mondale, Senator Baker, Speaker O'Neill,
Reverend Moomaw, and my fellow citizens.

To a few of us here today this is a solemn and most momentous occasion, and yet in the history of our nation it is a commonplace occurrence. The orderly transfer of authority as called for in the Constitution routinely takes place, as it has for almost two centuries, and few of us stop to think how unique we really are. In the eyes of many in the world, this every-four-year ceremony we accept as normal is nothing less than a miracle.

Mr. President, I want our fellow citizens to know how much you did to carry on this tradition. By your gracious cooperation in the transition process, you have shown a watching world that we are a united people pledged to maintaining a political system which guarantees individual liberty to a greater degree than any other, and I thank you and your people for all your help in maintaining the continuity which is the bulwark of our republic. The business of our nation goes forward. These United States are confronted with an economic affliction of great proportions. We suffer from the longest and one of the worst sustained inflations in our national history. It distorts our economic decisions, penalizes thrift, and crushes the struggling young and the fixed-income elderly alike. It threatens to shatter the lives of millions of our people.

Idle industries have cast workers into unemployment, human misery, and personal indignity. Those who do work

> Nancy Reagan watches her
> husband take the presidential
> oath of office at the Capitol
> in Washington, D.C.,
> January 20, 1981.

are denied a fair return for their labor by a tax system which penalizes successful achievement and keeps us from maintaining full productivity.

But great as our tax burden is, it has not kept pace with public spending. For decades we have piled deficit upon deficit, mortgaging our future and our children's future for the temporary convenience of the present. To continue this long trend is to guarantee tremendous social, cultural, political, and economic upheavals.

You and I, as individuals, can, by borrowing, live beyond our means, but for only a limited period of time. Why, then, should we think that collectively, as a nation, we're not bound by that same limitation? We must act today in order to preserve tomorrow. And let there be no misunderstanding: We are going to begin to act, beginning today. The economic ills we suffer have come upon us over several decades. They will not go away in days, weeks, or months, but they will go away. They will go away because we as Americans have the capacity now, as we've had in the past, to do whatever needs to be done to preserve this last and greatest bastion of freedom.

In this present crisis, government is not the solution to our problem; government is the problem. From time to time we've been tempted to believe that society has become too complex to be managed by self-rule, that government by an elite group is superior to government for, by, and of the people. Well, if no one among us is capable of governing himself, then who among us has the capacity to govern someone else? All of us together, in and out of government, must bear the burden. The solutions we seek must be equitable, with no one group singled out to pay a higher price.

We hear much of special interest groups. Well, our concern must be for a special interest group that has been too long neglected. It knows no sectional boundaries or ethnic and racial divisions, and it crosses political party lines. It is made up of men and women who raise our food, patrol our streets, man our mines and factories, teach our children, keep our homes, and heal us when we're sick—professionals, industrialists, shopkeepers, clerks, cabbies, and truck drivers. They are, in short, "we the people," this breed called Americans.

Well, this administration's objective will be a healthy, vigorous, growing economy that provides equal opportunities for all Americans, with no barriers born of bigotry or discrimination. Putting America back to work means

putting all Americans back to work. Ending inflation means freeing all Americans from the terror of runaway living costs. All must share in the productive work of this "new beginning," and all must share in the bounty of a revived economy. With the idealism and fair play which are the core of our system and our strength, we can have a strong and prosperous America, at peace with itself and the world.

So as we begin, let us take inventory. We are a nation that has a government—not the other way around. And this makes us special among the nations of the Earth. Our government has no power except that granted it by the people. It is time to check and reverse the growth of government, which shows signs of having grown beyond the consent of the governed.

President Reagan, having been sworn in as the fortieth president of the United States, gives his first inaugural address, January 20, 1981. First Lady Nancy Reagan is seated on the right in the first row next to Barbara Bush, wife of Vice President George Bush, who is sitting behind Reagan. House Speaker Thomas P. "Tip" O'Neill is to the president's right.

It is my intention to curb the size and influence of the federal establishment and to demand recognition of the distinction between the powers granted to the federal government and those reserved to the states or to the people. All of us need to be reminded that the federal government did not create the states; the states created the federal government.

Now, so there will be no misunderstanding, it's not my intention to do away with government. It is rather to make it work—work with us, not over us; to stand by our side, not ride on our back. Government can and must provide opportunity, not smother it; foster productivity, not stifle it.

If we look to the answer as to why for so many years we achieved so much, prospered as no other people on earth, it was because here in this land we unleashed the energy and individual genius of man to a greater extent than has ever been done before. Freedom and the dignity of the individual have been more available and assured here than in any other place on earth. The price for this freedom at times has been high, but we have never been unwilling to pay the price.

It is no coincidence that our present troubles parallel and are proportionate to the intervention and intrusion in our lives that result from unnecessary and excessive growth of government. It is time for us to realize that we're too great a nation to limit ourselves to small dreams. We're not, as some would have us believe, doomed to an inevitable decline. I do not believe in a fate that will fall on us no matter what we do. I do believe in a fate that will fall on us if we do nothing. So, with all the creative energy at our command, let us begin an era of national renewal. Let us renew our determination, our courage, and our strength. And let us renew our faith and our hope.

We have every right to dream heroic dreams. Those who say that we're in a time when there are no heroes, they just don't know where to look. You can see heroes every day going in and out of factory gates. Others, a handful in number, produce enough food to feed all of us and then the world beyond. You meet heroes across a counter, and they're on both sides of that counter. There are entrepreneurs with faith in themselves and faith in an idea who create new jobs, new wealth and opportunity. They're individuals and families whose taxes support the government and whose voluntary gifts support church, charity, culture, art, and education. Their patriotism is quiet, but deep. Their values sustain our national life.

Now, I have used the words *they* and *their* in speaking of these heroes. I could say *you* and *your*, because I'm addressing the heroes of whom I speak—you, the citizens of this blessed land. Your dreams, your hopes, your goals are going to be the dreams, the hopes, and the goals of this administration, so help me God.

We shall reflect the compassion that is so much a part of your makeup. How can we love our country and not love our countrymen; and loving them, reach out a hand when they fall, heal them when they're sick, and provide opportunity to make them self-sufficient so they will be equal in fact and not just in theory?

Can we solve the problems confronting us? Well, the answer is an unequivocal and emphatic yes. To paraphrase Winston Churchill, I did not take the oath I've just taken with the intention of presiding over the dissolution of the world's strongest economy.

In the days ahead I will propose removing the roadblocks that have slowed our economy and reduced productivity. Steps will be taken aimed at restoring the balance between the various levels of government. Progress may be slow, measured in inches and feet, not miles, but we will progress. It is time to reawaken this industrial giant, to get government back within its means, and to lighten our punitive tax burden. And these will be our first priorities, and on these principles there will be no compromise.

On the eve of our struggle for independence a man who might have been one of the greatest among the Founding Fathers, Dr. Joseph Warren, president of the Massachusetts Congress, said to his fellow Americans, "Our country is in danger, but not to be despaired of . . . On you depend the fortunes of America. You are to decide the important questions upon which rests the happiness and the liberty of millions yet unborn. Act worthy of yourselves." Well, I believe we, the Americans of today, are ready to act worthy of ourselves, ready to do what must be done to ensure happiness and liberty for ourselves, our children, and our children's children. And as we renew ourselves here in our own land, we will be seen as having greater strength throughout the world. We will again be the exemplar of freedom and a beacon of hope for those who do not now have freedom.

To those neighbors and allies who share our freedom, we will strengthen our historic ties and assure them of our support and firm commitment. We

The president and first lady,
and their extended families,
pose for the official inaugural
family photograph, 1981.

will match loyalty with loyalty. We will strive for mutually beneficial relations. We will not use our friendship to impose on their sovereignty, for our own sovereignty is not for sale. As for the enemies of freedom, those who are potential adversaries, they will be reminded that peace is the highest aspiration of the American people. We will negotiate for it, sacrifice for it; we will not surrender for it, now or ever.

Our forbearance should never be misunderstood. Our reluctance for conflict should not be misjudged as a failure of will. When action is required to preserve our national security, we will act. We will maintain sufficient strength to prevail if need be, knowing that if we do so, we have the best chance of never having to use that strength. Above all, we must realize that no arsenal or no weapon in the arsenals of the world is so formidable as the will and moral courage of free men and women. It is a weapon our adversaries in today's world do not have. It is a weapon that we as Americans do have. Let that be understood by those who practice terrorism and prey upon their neighbors. I'm told that tens of thousands of prayer meetings are being held on this day, and for that I'm deeply grateful. We are a nation under God, and I believe God intended for us to be free. It would be fitting and good, I think, if on each Inaugural Day in future years it should be declared a day of prayer.

This is the first time in our history that this ceremony has been held, as you've been told, on the West Front of the Capitol. Standing here, one faces a magnificent vista, opening up on the city's special beauty and history. At the end of this open mall are those shrines to the giants on whose shoulders we stand.

Directly in front of me, the monument to a monumental man, George Washington, father of our country. A man of humility who came to greatness reluctantly. He led Americans out of revolutionary victory into infant nationhood. Off to one side, the stately memorial to Thomas Jefferson. The Declaration of Independence flames with his eloquence. And then, beyond the Reflecting Pool, the dignified columns of the Lincoln Memorial. Whoever would understand in his heart the meaning of America will find it in the life of Abraham Lincoln.

Beyond those monuments to heroism is the Potomac River, and on the far shore the sloping hills of Arlington National Cemetery, with its row upon row of simple white markers bearing crosses or Stars of David. They add up to only a tiny fraction of the price that has been paid for our freedom. Each one of those markers is a monument to the kind of hero I spoke of earlier. Their lives ended in places called Belleau Wood, the Argonne, Omaha Beach, Salerno, and halfway around the world on Guadalcanal, Tarawa, Pork Chop Hill, the Chosin Reservoir, and in a hundred rice paddies and jungles of a place called Vietnam.

Under one such marker lies a young man, Martin Treptow, who left his job in a small-town barbershop in 1917 to go to France with the famed Rainbow Division. There, on the western front, he was killed trying to carry a message between battalions under heavy artillery fire.

We're told that on his body was found a diary. On the flyleaf under the heading "My Pledge," he had written these words: "America must win this war. Therefore I will work, I will save, I will sacrifice, I will endure, I will fight cheerfully and do my utmost, as if the issue of the whole struggle depended on me alone."

The crisis we are facing today does not require of us the kind of sacrifice that Martin Treptow and so many thousands of others were called upon to make. It does require, however, our best effort and our willingness to believe in ourselves and to believe in our capacity to perform great deeds, to believe that together with God's help we can and will resolve the problems which now confront us.

And after all, why shouldn't we believe that? We are Americans.

God bless you, and thank you.

Text of *Challenger* Disaster Address, January 28, 1986

The space shuttle Challenger *exploded just over a minute into its flight on January 28, 1986. President Reagan had been due to present the state of the union speech that night but instead spoke to the nation of the seven astronauts who had died that day.*

Ladies and gentlemen, I'd planned to speak to you tonight to report on the state of the union, but the events of earlier today have led me to change those plans. Today is a day for mourning and remembering. Nancy and I are pained to the core by the tragedy of the shuttle *Challenger*. We know we share this pain with all of the people of our country. This is truly a national loss.

Nineteen years ago, almost to the day, we lost three astronauts in a terrible accident on the ground. But we've never lost an astronaut in flight; we've never had a tragedy like this. And perhaps we've forgotten the courage it took for the crew of the shuttle; but they, the *Challenger* Seven, were aware of the dangers, but overcame them and did their jobs brilliantly. We mourn seven heroes: Michael Smith, Dick Scobee, Judith Resnik, Ronald McNair, Ellison Onizuka, Gregory Jarvis, and Christa McAuliffe. We mourn their loss as a nation together.

For the families of the seven, we cannot bear, as you do, the full impact of this tragedy. But we feel the loss, and we're thinking about you so very much. Your loved ones were daring and brave, and they had that special grace, that special spirit that says, "Give me a challenge and I'll meet it with joy." They had a hunger to explore the universe and discover its truths. They wished to serve, and they did. They served all of us.

> **"Touching the face of God."** The president in the Oval Office after addressing the nation about the explosion of the *Challenger* space shuttle, January 28, 1986.

We've grown used to wonders in this century. It's hard to dazzle us. But for twenty-five years the United States space program has been doing just that. We've grown used to the idea of space, and perhaps we forget that we've only just begun. We're still pioneers. They, the members of the *Challenger* crew, were pioneers.

And I want to say something to the schoolchildren of America who were watching the live coverage of the shuttle's takeoff. I know it is hard to understand, but sometimes painful things like this happen. It's all part of the process of exploration and discovery. It's all part of taking a chance and expanding man's horizons. The future doesn't belong to the fainthearted; it belongs to the brave. The *Challenger* crew was pulling us into the future, and we'll continue to follow them.

I've always had great faith in and respect for our space program, and what happened today does nothing to diminish it. We don't hide our space program. We don't keep secrets and cover things up. We do it all up front and in public. That's the way freedom is, and we wouldn't change it for a minute. We'll continue our quest in space. There will be more shuttle flights and more shuttle crews and yes, more volunteers, more civilians, more teachers in space. Nothing ends here; our hopes and our journeys continue.

I want to add that I wish I could talk to every man and woman who works for NASA or who worked on this mission and tell them: "Your dedication and professionalism have moved and impressed us for decades. And we know of your anguish. We share it."

There's a coincidence today. On this day 390 years ago, the great explorer Sir Francis Drake died aboard ship off the coast of Panama. In his lifetime the great frontiers were the oceans, and a historian later said, "He lived by the sea, died on it, and was buried in it." Well, today we can say of the *Challenger* crew: Their dedication was, like Drake's, complete.

The crew of the space shuttle *Challenger* honored us by the manner in which they lived their lives. We will never forget them, nor the last time we saw them, this morning, as they prepared for their journey and waved good-bye and "slipped the surly bonds of earth" to "touch the face of God."

TEXT OF BRANDENBURG GATE SPEECH, JUNE 12, 1987

The wall dividing East and West Berlin symbolized the cold war. Standing before the wall at the historic Brandenburg Gate, within earshot of the eastern part of the city, President Reagan invited his Soviet counterpart to "tear down this wall."

———————

Thank you very much.

Chancellor Kohl, Governing Mayor Diepgen, ladies and gentlemen: Twenty-four years ago, President John F. Kennedy visited Berlin, speaking to the people of this city and the world at the City Hall. Well, since then two other presidents have come, each in his turn, to Berlin. And today I myself make my second visit to your city.

We come to Berlin, we American presidents, because it's our duty to speak in this place of freedom. But I must confess, we're drawn here by other things as well: by the feeling of history in this city, more than five hundred years older than our own nation; by the beauty of the Grunewald and the Tiergarten; most of all, by your courage and determination. Perhaps the composer Paul Lincke understood something about American presidents. You see, like so many presidents before me, I come here today because wherever I go, whatever I do: *Ich hab noch einen Koffer in Berlin.* [I still have a suitcase in Berlin.]

Our gathering today is being broadcast throughout Western Europe and North America. I understand that it is being seen and heard as well in the East. To those listening throughout Eastern Europe, a special word: Although I cannot be with you, I address my remarks to you just as surely as to those standing here before me. For I join you, as I join your fellow countrymen in the West, in this firm, this unalterable belief: *Es gibt nur ein Berlin.* [There is only one Berlin.]

Behind me stands a wall that encircles the free sectors of this city, part of a vast system of barriers that divides the entire continent of Europe. From the Baltic south, those barriers cut across Germany in a gash of barbed wire, concrete, dog runs, and guard towers. Farther south, there may be no visible, no obvious wall. But there remain armed guards and checkpoints all the same—still a restriction on the right to travel, still an instrument to impose upon ordinary men and women the will of a totalitarian state. Yet it is here in Berlin where the wall emerges most clearly; here, cutting across your city, where the news photos and the television screen have imprinted this brutal division of a continent upon the mind of the world. Standing before the Brandenburg Gate, every man is a German, separated from his fellow men. Every man is a Berliner, forced to look upon a scar.

President von Weizsäcker has said, "The German question is open as long as the Brandenburg Gate is closed." Today I say: As long as the gate is closed, as long as this scar of a wall is permitted to stand, it is not the German question alone that remains open, but the question of freedom for all mankind. Yet I do not come here to lament. For I find in Berlin a message of hope, even in the shadow of this wall, a message of triumph.

In this season of spring in 1945, the people of Berlin emerged from their air-raid shelters to find devastation. Thousands of miles away, the people of the United States reached out to help. And in 1947 Secretary of State—as you've been told—George Marshall announced the creation of what would become known as the Marshall Plan. Speaking precisely forty years ago this month, he said: "Our policy is directed not against any country or doctrine, but against hunger, poverty, desperation, and chaos."

In the Reichstag a few moments ago, I saw a display commemorating this fortieth anniversary of the Marshall Plan. I was struck by the sign on a burnt-out, gutted structure that was being rebuilt. I understand that Berliners of my own generation can remember seeing signs like it dotted throughout the western sectors of the city. The sign read simply: "The Marshall Plan is helping here to strengthen the free world." A strong, free world in the West, that dream became real. Japan rose from ruin to become an economic giant. Italy, France, Belgium—virtually every nation in Western Europe saw political and economic rebirth; the European Community was founded.

ALLIED
CHECKPOINT
CHARLIE

ACHTUNG!

YOU ARE LEAVING
THE
AMERICAN S
SIE VERLAS
AMERIKANIS
SEKTOR

In West Germany and here in Berlin, there took place an economic miracle, the *Wirtschaftswunder*. Adenauer, Erhard, Reuter, and other leaders understood the practical importance of liberty—that just as truth can flourish only when the journalist is given freedom of speech, so prosperity can come about only when the farmer and businessman enjoy economic freedom. The German leaders reduced tariffs, expanded free trade, lowered taxes. From 1950 to 1960 alone, the standard of living in West Germany and Berlin doubled.

Where four decades ago there was rubble, today in West Berlin there is the greatest industrial output of any city in Germany—busy office blocks, fine homes and apartments, proud avenues, and the spreading lawns of parkland. Where a city's culture seemed to have been destroyed, today there are two great universities, orchestras and an opera, countless theaters, and

On an earlier visit to the Berlin Wall, to the famous Checkpoint Charlie, June 1982. To Reagan's right is Berlin mayor Richard von Weizsäcker; to his left, West German chancellor Helmut Schmidt.

museums. Where there was want, today there's abundance—food, clothing, automobiles—the wonderful goods of the Ku'damm. From devastation, from utter ruin, you Berliners have, in freedom, rebuilt a city that once again ranks as one of the greatest on earth. The Soviets may have had other plans. But, my friends, there were a few things the Soviets didn't count on— *Berliner Herz, Berliner Humor, ja, und Berliner Schnauze.* [Berliner heart, Berliner humor, yes, and a Berliner "mouth."]

In the 1950s, Khrushchev predicted: "We will bury you." But in the West today, we see a free world that has achieved a level of prosperity and well-being unprecedented in all human history. In the communist world, we see failure, technological backwardness, declining standards of health, even want of the most basic kind—too little food. Even today, the Soviet Union still cannot feed itself. After these four decades, then, there stands before the entire world one great and inescapable conclusion: Freedom leads to prosperity. Freedom replaces the ancient hatreds among the nations with comity and peace. Freedom is the victor.

And now the Soviets themselves may, in a limited way, be coming to understand the importance of freedom. We hear much from Moscow about a new policy of reform and openness. Some political prisoners have been released. Certain foreign news broadcasts are no longer being jammed. Some economic enterprises have been permitted to operate with greater freedom from state control.

Are these the beginnings of profound changes in the Soviet state? Or are they token gestures, intended to raise false hopes in the West, or to strengthen the Soviet system without changing it? We welcome change and openness; for we believe that freedom and security go together, that the advance of human liberty can only strengthen the cause of world peace. There is one sign the Soviets can make that would be unmistakable, that would advance dramatically the cause of freedom and peace.

General Secretary Gorbachev, if you seek peace, if you seek prosperity for the Soviet Union and Eastern Europe, if you seek liberalization: Come here to this gate! Mr. Gorbachev, open this gate! Mr. Gorbachev, tear down this wall!

I understand the fear of war and the pain of division that afflict this continent—and I pledge to you my country's efforts to help overcome these burdens. To be sure, we in the West must resist Soviet expansion. So we must maintain defenses of unassailable strength. Yet we seek peace; so we must strive to reduce arms on both sides.

Beginning ten years ago, the Soviets challenged the Western alliance with a grave new threat: hundreds of new and more deadly SS-20 nuclear missiles, capable of striking every capital in Europe. The Western alliance responded by committing itself to a counter-deployment unless the Soviets agreed to negotiate a better solution; namely, the elimination of such weapons on both sides. For many months, the Soviets refused to bargain in earnestness. As the alliance in turn prepared to go forward with its counter-deployment, there were difficult days—days of protests like those during my 1982 visit to this city—and the Soviets later walked away from the table.

But through it all, the alliance held firm. And I invite those who protested then—I invite those who protest today—to mark this fact: Because we remained strong, the Soviets came back to the table. And because we remained strong, today we have within reach the possibility, not merely of limiting the growth of arms, but of eliminating, for the first time, an entire class of nuclear weapons from the face of the earth.

As I speak, NATO ministers are meeting in Iceland to review the progress of our proposals for eliminating these weapons. At the talks in Geneva, we have also proposed deep cuts in strategic offensive weapons. And the Western allies have likewise made far-reaching proposals to reduce the danger of conventional war and to place a total ban on chemical weapons.

While we pursue these arms reductions, I pledge to you that we will maintain the capacity to deter Soviet aggression at any level at which it might occur. And in cooperation with many of our allies, the United States is pursuing the Strategic Defense Initiative—research to base deterrence not on the threat of offensive retaliation, but on defenses that truly defend; on systems, in short, that will not target populations, but shield them. By these means we seek to increase the safety of Europe and all the world. But we must remember a crucial fact: East and West do not mistrust each other because we are armed; we are armed because we mistrust each other. And our differences are not about weapons but about liberty. When President Kennedy spoke at the City Hall those twenty-four years ago, freedom was encircled, Berlin was under siege. And today, despite all the pressures upon this city, Berlin stands secure in its liberty. And freedom itself is transforming the globe.

In the Philippines, in South and Central America, democracy has been given a rebirth. Throughout the Pacific, free markets are working miracle after miracle of economic growth. In the industrialized nations, a technological revolution is taking place—a revolution marked by rapid, dramatic advances in computers and telecommunications.

In Europe, only one nation and those it controls refuse to join the community of freedom. Yet in this age of redoubled economic growth, of information and innovation, the Soviet Union faces a choice: It must make fundamental changes or it will become obsolete.

Today thus represents a moment of hope. We in the West stand ready to cooperate with the East to promote true openness, to break down barriers that separate people, to create a safe, freer world. And surely there is no better place than Berlin, the meeting place of East and West, to make a start. Free people of Berlin: Today, as in the past, the United States stands for the strict observance and full implementation of all parts of the Four Power Agreement of 1971. Let us use this occasion, the 750th anniversary of this city, to usher in a new era, to seek a still fuller, richer life for the Berlin of the future. Together, let us maintain and develop the ties between the Federal Republic and the Western sectors of Berlin, which is permitted by the 1971 agreement.

And I invite Mr. Gorbachev: Let us work to bring the Eastern and Western parts of the city closer together, so that all the inhabitants of all Berlin can enjoy the benefits that come with life in one of the great cities of the world.

To open Berlin still further to all Europe, East and West, let us expand the vital air access to this city, finding ways of making commercial air service to Berlin more convenient, more comfortable, and more economical. We look to the day when West Berlin can become one of the chief aviation hubs in all central Europe.

With our French and British partners, the United States is prepared to help bring international meetings to Berlin. It would be only fitting for Berlin to serve as the site of United

Nations meetings, or world conferences on human rights and arms control or other issues that call for international cooperation.

There is no better way to establish hope for the future than to enlighten young minds, and we would be honored to sponsor summer youth exchanges, cultural events, and other programs for young Berliners from the East. Our French and British friends, I'm certain, will do the same. And it's my hope that an authority can be found in East Berlin to sponsor visits from young people of the Western sectors.

One final proposal, one close to my heart: Sport represents a source of enjoyment and ennoblement, and you may have noted that the Republic of Korea—South Korea—has offered to permit certain events of the 1988 Olympics to take place in the North. International sports competitions of all kinds could take place in both parts of this city. And what better way to demonstrate to the world the openness of this city than to offer in some future year to hold the Olympic games here in Berlin, East and West? In these four decades, as I have said, you Berliners have built a great city. You've done so in spite of threats—the Soviet attempts to impose the East-mark, the blockade. Today the city thrives in spite of the challenges implicit in the very presence of this wall. What keeps you here? Certainly there's a great deal to be said for your fortitude, for your defiant courage. But I believe there's something deeper, something that involves Berlin's whole look and feel and way of life—not mere sentiment. No one could live long in Berlin without being completely disabused of illusions. Something instead that has seen the difficulties of life in Berlin but chosen to accept them, that continues to build this good and proud city in contrast to a surrounding totalitarian presence that refuses to release human energies or aspirations. Something that speaks with a powerful voice of affirmation, that says yes to this city, yes to the future, yes to freedom. In a word, I would submit that what keeps you in Berlin is love—love both profound and abiding.

Perhaps this gets to the root of the matter, to the most fundamental distinction of all between East and West. The totalitarian world produces backwardness because it does such violence to the spirit, thwarting the human impulse to create, to enjoy, to worship. The totalitarian world finds even symbols of love and of worship an affront. Years ago, before the East Germans began rebuilding their churches, they erected a secular structure:

the television tower at Alexanderplatz. Virtually ever since, the authorities have been working to correct what they view as the tower's one major flaw, treating the glass sphere at the top with paints and chemicals of every kind. Yet even today when the sun strikes that sphere—that sphere that towers over all Berlin—the light makes the sign of the cross. There in Berlin, like the city itself, symbols of love, symbols of worship, cannot be suppressed.

As I looked out a moment ago from the Reichstag, that embodiment of German unity, I noticed words crudely spray-painted upon the wall, perhaps by a young Berliner: "This wall will fall. Beliefs become reality." Yes, across Europe, this wall will fall. For it cannot withstand faith; it cannot withstand truth. The wall cannot withstand freedom.

And I would like, before I close, to say one word. I have read and I have been questioned since I've been here about certain demonstrations against my coming. And I would like to say just one thing, and to those who demonstrate so, I wonder if they have ever asked themselves that if they should have the kind of government they apparently seek, no one would ever be able to do what they're doing again.

Thank you and God bless you all.

In Red Square, with Lenin's tomb behind them, U.S. president Ronald Reagan and Soviet leader Mikhail Gorbachev kiss a baby for the camera, Moscow, May 31, 1988. Between Gorbachev and Reagan are the Soviet interpreter Pavel Palazhchenko and Reagan's chief of staff Howard Baker.

Text of Farewell Address to the Nation, January 11, 1989

A few days before George H. W. Bush's inauguration,
Ronald Reagan spoke to the nation for the last time from
the Oval Office and talked about the state of the "shining
city upon a hill" after eight years in his care.

———

This is the thirty-fourth time I'll speak to you from the Oval Office and the last. We've been together eight years now, and soon it'll be time for me to go. But before I do, I wanted to share some thoughts, some of which I've been saving for a long time.

It's been the honor of my life to be your president. So many of you have written the past few weeks to say thanks, but I could say as much to you. Nancy and I are grateful for the opportunity you gave us to serve.

One of the things about the presidency is that you're always somewhat apart. You spend a lot of time going by too fast in a car someone else is driving, and seeing the people through tinted glass—the parents holding up a child, and the wave you saw too late and couldn't return. And so many times I wanted to stop and reach out from behind the glass, and connect. Well, maybe I can do a little of that tonight.

People ask how I feel about leaving. And the fact is, "parting is such sweet sorrow." The sweet part is California, and the ranch and freedom. The sorrow—the good-byes, of course, and leaving this beautiful place.

You know, down the hall and up the stairs from this office is the part of the White House where the president and his family live. There are a few favorite windows I have up there that I like to stand and look out of early in the morning. The view is over the grounds here to the Washington Monument, and then the Mall and the Jefferson Memorial. But on mornings when the humidity is low, you

President Reagan in his Oval Office study, December 1987.

During his presidency, Ronald Reagan loved to relax at his "Ranch in the Sky"—Rancho del Cielo. Reagan was often pictured in vigorous activity, chopping wood or, as in this 1982 photograph, clearing brush with a chain saw.

can see past the Jefferson to the river, the Potomac, and the Virginia shore. Someone said that's the view Lincoln had when he saw the smoke rising from the Battle of Bull Run. I see more prosaic things: the grass on the banks, the morning traffic as people make their way to work, now and then a sailboat on the river.

I've been thinking a bit at that window. I've been reflecting on what the past eight years have meant and mean. And the image that comes to mind like a refrain is a nautical one—a small story about a big ship, and a refugee and a sailor. It was back in the early eighties, at the height of the boat people. And the sailor was hard at work on the carrier *Midway*, which was patrolling the South China Sea. The sailor, like most American servicemen, was young, smart, and fiercely observant. The crew spied on the horizon a leaky little boat. And crammed inside were refugees from Indochina hoping to get to America. The *Midway* sent a small launch to bring them to the ship and safety. As the refugees made their way through the choppy seas, one spied the sailor on deck and stood up and called out to him. He yelled, "Hello, American sailor. Hello, freedom man."

A small moment with a big meaning, a moment the sailor, who wrote it in a letter, couldn't get out of his mind. And when I saw it, neither could I. Because that's what it was to be an American in the 1980s. We stood, again, for freedom. I know we always have, but in the past few years the world again, and in a way, we ourselves rediscovered it.

It's been quite a journey this decade, and we held together through some stormy seas. And at the end, together we are reaching our destination.

The fact is, from Grenada to the Washington and Moscow summits, from the recession of '81 to '82, to the expansion that began in late '82 and continues to this day, we've made a difference. The way I see it, there were two great triumphs, two things that I'm proudest of. One is the economic recovery, in which the people of America created—and filled—19 million new jobs. The other is the recovery of our morale. America is respected again in the world and looked to for leadership.

Something that happened to me a few years ago reflects some of this. It was back in 1981, and I was attending my first big economic summit, which was held that year in Canada. The meeting place rotates among the member countries. The opening meeting was a formal dinner for the heads of government of the seven industrialized nations. Now, I sat there like the new kid in school and listened, and it was all François this and Helmut that. They dropped titles and spoke to one another on a first-name basis. Well, at one point I sort of leaned in and said, "My name's Ron." Well, in that same year, we began the actions we felt would ignite an economic comeback—cut taxes and regulation, started to cut spending. And soon the recovery began.

Two years later another economic summit, with pretty much the same cast. At the big opening meeting we all got together, and all of a sudden, just for a moment, I saw that everyone was just sitting there looking at me. And one of them broke the silence. "Tell us about the American miracle," he said.

Well, back in 1980, when I was running for president, it was all so different. Some pundits said our programs would result in catastrophe. Our views on foreign affairs would cause war. Our plans for the economy would cause inflation to soar and bring about economic collapse. I even remember one highly respected economist saying, back in 1982, that "the engines of economic growth have shut down here, and they're likely to stay that way for years to come." Well, he and the other opinion leaders were wrong. The fact is, what they called radical was really right. What they called dangerous was just desperately needed.

And in all of that time I won a nickname, "The Great Communicator." But I never thought it was my style or the words I used that made a difference: It was the content. I wasn't a great communicator, but I communicated great things, and they didn't spring full bloom from my brow, they came from the heart of a great nation—from our experience, our wisdom, and our belief in principles that have guided us for two centuries. They called it the Reagan revolution. Well, I'll accept that, but for me it always seemed more like the great rediscovery, a rediscovery of our values and our common sense.

Common sense told us that when you put a big tax on something, the people will produce less of it. So we cut the people's tax rates, and the people produced more than ever before. The economy bloomed like a plant that had been cut back and could now grow quicker and stronger. Our economic

program brought about the longest peacetime expansion in our history: real family income up, the poverty rate down, entre-preneurship booming, and an explosion in research and new technology. We're exporting more than ever because American industry became more competitive, and at the same time, we summoned the national will to knock down protectionist walls abroad instead of erecting them at home. Common sense also told us that to preserve the peace, we'd have to become strong again after years of weakness and confusion. So we rebuilt our defenses, and this New Year we toasted the new peacefulness around the globe. Not only have the superpowers actually begun to reduce their stockpiles of nuclear weapons—and hope for even more progress is bright—but the regional conflicts that rack the globe are also beginning to cease. The Persian Gulf is

In a bill-signing ceremony at the White House Rose Garden on July 17, 1984, President Reagan raises the drinking age to twenty-one. Among those in attendance are Transportation Secretary Elizabeth Dole and, next to Reagan, the founder of pressure group Mothers Against Drunk Driving, Candy Lightner.

no longer a war zone. The Soviets are leaving Afghanistan. The Vietnamese are preparing to pull out of Cambodia, and an American-mediated accord will soon send 50,000 Cuban troops home from Angola.

The lesson of all this was, of course, that because we're a great nation, our challenges seem complex. It will always be this way. But as long as we remember our first principles and believe in ourselves, the future will always be ours. And something else we learned: Once you begin a great movement, there's no telling where it will end. We meant to change a nation, and instead, we changed a world.

Countries across the globe are turning to free markets and free speech and turning away from ideologies of the past. For them, the great rediscovery of the 1980s has been that, lo and behold, the moral way of government is the practical way of government: Democracy, the profoundly good, is also the profoundly productive.

When you've got to the point when you can celebrate the anniversaries of your thirty-ninth birthday, you can sit back sometimes, review your life, and see it flowing before you. For me there was a fork in the river, and it was right in the middle of my life. I never meant to go into politics. It wasn't my intention when I was young. But I was raised to believe you had to pay your way for the blessings bestowed on you. I was happy with my career in the entertainment world, but I ultimately went into politics because I wanted to protect something precious.

Ours was the first revolution in the history of mankind that truly reversed the course of government, and with three little words: "We the people." "We the people" tell the government what to do, it doesn't tell us. "We the people" are the driver, the government is the car. And we decide where it should go and by what route and how fast. Almost all the world's constitutions are documents in which governments tell the people what their privileges are. Our Constitution is a document in which "we the people" tell the government what it is allowed to do. "We the people" are free. This belief has been the underlying basis for everything I've tried to do these past eight years.

But back in the 1960s, when I began, it seemed to me that we'd begun reversing the order of things—that through more and more rules and regulations and confiscatory taxes, the government was taking more of our money, more of our options, and more of our freedom. I went into politics

in part to put up my hand and say, "Stop." I was a citizen politician, and it seemed the right thing for a citizen to do.

I think we have stopped a lot of what needed stopping. And I hope we have once again reminded people that man is not free unless government is limited. There's a clear cause and effect here that is as neat and predictable as a law of physics: As government expands, liberty contracts.

Nothing is less free than pure communism, and yet we have, the past few years, forged a satisfying new closeness with the Soviet Union. I've been asked if this isn't a gamble, and my answer is no, because we're basing our actions not on words but deeds. The detente of the 1970s was based not on actions but

The president and first lady are photographed on the White House lawn in December 1986 together with their King Charles spaniel, Rex.

promises. They'd promise to treat their own people and the people of the world better. But the gulag was still the gulag, and the state was still expansionist, and they still waged proxy wars in Africa, Asia, and Latin America.

Well, this time, so far, it's different. President Gorbachev has brought about some internal democratic reforms and begun the withdrawal from Afghanistan. He has also freed prisoners whose names I've given him every time we've met.

But life has a way of reminding you of big things through small incidents. Once, during the heady days of the Moscow summit, Nancy and I decided to break off from the entourage one afternoon to visit the shops on Arbat Street—that's a little street just off Moscow's main shopping area. Even though our visit was a surprise, every Russian there immediately recognized us and called out our names and reached for our hands. We were just about swept away by the warmth. You could almost feel the possibilities in all that joy. But within seconds, a KGB detail pushed their way toward us and began pushing and shoving the people in the crowd. It was an interesting moment. It reminded me that while the man on the street in the Soviet Union yearns for peace, the government is communist. And those who run it are communists, and that means we and they view such issues as freedom and human rights very differently.

We must keep up our guard, but we must also continue to work together to lessen and eliminate tension and mistrust. My view is that President Gorbachev is different from previous Soviet leaders. I think he knows some of the things wrong with his society and is trying to fix them. We wish him well. And we'll continue to work to make sure that the Soviet Union that eventually emerges from this process is a less threatening one. What it all boils down to is this. I want the new closeness to continue. And it will, as long as we make it clear that we will continue to act in a certain way as long as they continue to act in a helpful manner. If and when they don't, at first pull your punches. If they persist, pull the plug. It's still trust but verify. It's still play, but cut the cards. It's still watch closely. And don't be afraid to see what you see.

I've been asked if I have any regrets. Well, I do. The deficit is one. I've been talking a great deal about that lately,

A formally dressed president and first lady relax in the Yellow Oval Room in the White House as they wait for President Miguel de la Madrid Hurtado of Mexico, May 15, 1984.

but tonight isn't for arguments. And I'm going to hold my tongue. But an observation: I've had my share of victories in the Congress, but what few people noticed is that I never won anything you didn't win for me. They never saw my troops, they never saw Reagan's regiments, the American people. You won every battle with every call you made and letter you wrote demanding action. Well, action is still needed. If we're to finish the job, Reagan's regiments will have to become the Bush brigades. Soon he'll be the chief, and he'll need you every bit as much as I did. Finally, there is a great tradition of warnings in presidential farewells, and I've got one that's been on my mind for some time. But oddly enough it starts with one of the things I'm proudest of in the past eight years: the resurgence of national pride that I called the new patriotism. This national feeling is good, but it won't count for much and it won't last unless it's grounded in thoughtfulness and knowledge.

An informed patriotism is what we want. And are we doing a good enough job teaching our children what America is and what she represents in the long history of the world? Those of us who are over thirty-five or so years of age grew up in a different America. We were taught, very directly, what it means to be an American. And we absorbed, almost in the air, a love of country and an appreciation of its institutions. If you didn't get these things from your family, you got them from the neighborhood, from the father down the street who fought in Korea or the family who lost someone at Anzio. Or you could get a sense of patriotism from school. And if all else failed, you could get a sense of patriotism from popular culture. The movies celebrated democratic values and implicitly reinforced the idea that America was special. TV was like that, too, through the mid-sixties.

But now, we're about to enter the nineties, and some things have changed. Younger parents aren't sure that an unambivalent appreciation of America is the right thing to teach modern children. And as for those who create the popular culture, well-grounded patriotism is no longer the style. Our spirit is back, but we haven't reinstitutionalized it. We've got to do a better job of getting across that America is freedom—freedom of speech, freedom of religion, freedom of enterprise. And freedom is special and rare. It's fragile; it needs protection.

So we've got to teach history based not on what's in fashion but what's important: Why the Pilgrims came here, who Jimmy Doolittle was, and what

those thirty seconds over Tokyo meant. You know, four years ago on the fortieth anniversary of D-day, I read a letter from a young woman writing of her late father, who'd fought on Omaha Beach. Her name was Lisa Zanatta Henn, and she said, "We will always remember, we will never forget what the boys of Normandy did." Well, let's help her keep her word. If we forget what we did, we won't know who we are. I'm warning of an eradication of the American memory that could result, ultimately, in an erosion of the American spirit. Let's start with some basics: more attention to American history and a greater emphasis on civic ritual. And let me offer lesson number one about America: All great change in America begins at the dinner table. So tomorrow night in the kitchen I hope the talking begins. And children, if your parents haven't been teaching you what it means to be an American, let 'em know and nail 'em on it. That would be a very American thing to do.

And that's about all I have to say tonight. Except for one thing. The past few days when I've been at that window upstairs, I've thought a bit of the "shining city upon a hill." The phrase comes from John Winthrop, who wrote it to describe the America he imagined. What he imagined was important because he was an early Pilgrim, an early freedom man. He journeyed here on what today we'd call a little wooden boat; and like the other Pilgrims, he was looking for a home that would be free.

I've spoken of the shining city all my political life, but I don't know if I ever quite communicated what I saw when I said it. But in my mind it was a tall proud city built on rocks stronger than oceans, windswept, God-blessed, and teeming with people of all kinds living in harmony and peace, a city with free ports that hummed with commerce and creativity, and if there had to be city walls, the walls had doors and the doors were open to anyone with the will and the heart to get here. That's how I saw it and see it still.

And how stands the city on this winter night? More prosperous, more secure, and happier than it was eight years ago. But more than that; after two hundred years, two centuries, she still stands strong and true on the granite ridge, and her glow has held steady no matter what storm. And she's still a beacon, still a magnet for all who must have freedom, for all the pilgrims from all the lost places who are hurtling through the darkness, toward home.

We've done our part. And as I walk off into the city streets, a final word to the men and women of the Reagan revolution, the men and women across America who for eight years did the work that brought America back. My friends: We did it. We weren't just marking time. We made a difference. We made the city stronger. We made the city freer, and we left her in good hands. All in all, not bad, not bad at all.

And so, good-bye, God bless you, and God bless the United States of America.

The Reagans walk to a helicopter after taking their leave of the Capitol and Washington, D.C., January 20, 1989.

PART THREE

A LIFE
AND A LEGACY

RONNIE AND NANCY

by Mike Wallace

Ronald Reagan deferred to me just once—on the subject of his beloved wife Nancy. During an early interview I asked him, rather foolishly, if she was his Lady Bird. "Nooo," he said, smiling, "she's no Lady Bird. You've known her longer than I have, so . . ." And he let it go at that.

Fact is, I've known her since her mother, Edie Davis, introduced us back in the forties in Chicago. In a short televised floor conversation at a GOP convention, I'd complimented Edie on the proper political wife Nancy had become. "Well, you helped me raise her," Edie inaccurately replied.

Nancy and her mother adored each other. Edie was earthy, even bawdy, hilariously funny and wonderfully warm. But the daughter she raised, I remember as proper, white-gloved and black-patent-leather-shod, her Peter Pan collars seldom askew. As I grew to know her, I liked her for her candor, her political insights, and strangely, for her vulnerability. Most political wives are thicker-skinned than she. She was surely no Barbara Bush.

Beyond that I admired the tigress in Nancy when she felt her "Ronnie" being misapprehended, or that his colleagues were in her eyes less than totally loyal to him. I used to talk to her regularly on the telephone from New York during her White House years. Our conversations, candid on both sides, were mutually understood to be off the record, and dealt mainly with political gossip and family affairs. (My son Chris was NBC's White House correspondent during that time.) And it was a joke between Nancy and me during those years (an unfunny joke to me) that not once did I get an "inside" story for *60 Minutes*, although I did get a series of interviews with the president along the way.

Even today, unhappily, as I've made plain to her, when she had some news to make news herself, as in the case of her opposition to President Bush's views on stem cell research, she has gone elsewhere to vent her differences with the president.

> **Ronald and Nancy Reagan on a boat in California, August 1964.**

Down the years, I've come to understand better the role she played with her husband. For instance, I've nothing concrete to cite in support of what I believe, but I have more than a hunch that during his second term she decided she was going to push him to make sure he would be recognized as a peacemaker along with his Soviet counterpart, Mikhail Gorbachev. For President Reagan, the Soviet Union was no longer going to be that "evil empire." Of course, Nancy Reagan would be the last to take any credit for the move to détente, but Gorbachev himself has made it clear that he believes her contribution was critical to changing her husband's perception of U.S.–Russian relations.

First ladies have a tough job, not least because they are always the object of scrutiny by those of us who believe it's our job to do just that: to get behind the façade. So they have to be keepers of secrets, diplomats, objects of speculation and sometimes of scorn, lightning rods, and obviously, presidential advisors.

Nancy Reagan, after the White House years and the fifteen difficult years beyond, has finally been recognized as one of the finest.

I'm proud that for half a century she's been my friend.

People, June 21, 2004

Waiting . . . and the End

by Patti Davis

On June 3 Patti Davis wrote for People *about the*
final days of her father's illness. Just two days later
Ronald Reagan passed away, and she added a sad coda.

My father is dying. Only a few days left now. Maybe a week. Maybe his soul is already gone. It looks like that—blue chalk eyes, more like a child's drawing than real eyes. No life in them, just existence.

It's been ten years since the diagnosis. Alzheimer's. A disease that arrives with death as its soulmate. I thought I was prepared. So many waves of grief have crashed over me during these years. But now I think there is another diving-down place that's still waiting for me. Two days ago my father's eyes stopped opening at all, his hand is as pale as the blanket covering him, and sometimes his breath just stops as seconds pass by and I wonder and hold my own breath. My father is dying and it feels like I've never thought about it before. Even though I've been living with the thought for a decade.

My father's voice fell silent weeks ago. Until then the sound of his voice hummed through the room sometimes—not with words, but maybe they were words to him. I said to my mother, maybe he's getting us used to the silence. She lives with all that silence, with the ticking by of minutes and the knowledge that death has to be better than ragged breathing and chalk blue eyes.

Her husband is dying. The man she loved for fifty-two years. Here is a snapshot of the waiting: A daughter holding her mother while she weeps, tears staining skin, a body shaking with so much pain you think if you were at the center of the earth you could probably feel it. My mother is tiny, her weight against me light, the back of her head is cupped in my hand. But her grief is huge and so heavy it pulls on the joints of my body. It will be okay, I tell her. But I have no idea if it will be.

His death will be a big unwieldy one—a world event. Press stories and news specials and foreign dignitaries arriving in America in black clothes with typed-up eulogies in their pockets. We will grab onto the massive grief around us and go home at night to the shape of grief inside us.

JUNE 6 My father has died. Five of us were there—my mother, Ron, me, the doctor, and the Irish nurse whose lilting voice always made him smile. We waited through the foggy morning into the midday sunlight. An intimate vigil, a bond formed that no one will forget. The room was filled with whispers, shared stories, soft laughter over fond memories. Silence, as we measured my father's breathing.

ABOVE: **Young Patricia and her father playing in the pool at their home in Pacific Palisades, California, 1966.**

OPPOSITE: **In 1992, Maureen Reagan ran for Congress. At a rally in Redondo Beach, California, Nancy applauds and Ronald Reagan hugs his daughter. The Reagans' son Ron is partly obscured behind his father.**

At the last moment, when his breathing told us this was it, he opened his eyes and looked straight at my mother. Eyes that hadn't opened for days did, and they weren't chalky or vague. They were clear and blue and full of love, and then they closed with his last breath. If a death can be lovely, his was. The greatest gift you could have given me, my mother managed to say to him through tears, through "I love you," through the towering beauty of that last moment. The hush in the room broken then by quiet crying.

The world turns pages of my father's life and wrestles with his death. There seems to be no other news story. A world event as we knew it would be. It used to be hard to share my father with a whole nation. Now you'd

have to be the most selfish person in the world not to take comfort from the support of so many.

Yet for me his death is simply this: One last moment of startling life, a memory seared into our hearts, the one antidote to the sorrow that will stream on with no end in sight. Death is eyes closing for the last time and other eyes opening—morning after morning—wondering if this will be the day when it gets easier.

My father told me when I was small that I didn't need to stand on my toes to touch God, because He is everywhere. He was right; God was in that room. In his last moment my father taught me that there is nothing stronger than love between two people. It reaches past death and cradles hearts that weep. The last thing he did in this world was to show my mother how entwined their souls are . . . and it was everything.

Newsweek, June 14, 2004

AMERICAN DREAMER

by Jon Meacham; with Andrew Murr, Eleanor Clift, Tamara Lipper, Karen Breslau, and Jennifer Ordonez

His timing, as always, was perfect.

Almost exactly twenty years after he stood before the aging soldiers of D-day on the cliffs of Normandy, saluting the warriors who had saved democracy, Ronald Reagan died quietly in his house on St. Cloud Drive in Bel Air last Saturday, ending his long and noble battle against Alzheimer's disease. "It was very peaceful," a family member told *Newsweek*. "It was time."

Word of Reagan's death came as the world was once again commemorating the Allied victory over Nazi tyranny. As presidents and princes, old soldiers and sailors, widows and grandchildren gathered on those same windswept beaches last weekend, they, and America, were hearing Reagan's words as they mourned his death. "These are the boys of Pointe du Hoc," Reagan had said on June 6, 1984, hailing the Rangers who helped spearhead the liberation. "These are the men who took the cliffs." Grown men wept that day in 1984; Reagan's voice caught with genuine emotion. "The men of Normandy had faith that what they were doing was right," he said, "faith that they fought for all humanity, faith that a just God would grant them mercy on this beachhead—or on the next."

He spoke with such grace, such conviction and such power that only the most cynical observers recalled that Reagan himself had spent World War II in Hollywood, making training films. That day at Normandy—and all the other days of his remarkable public life—Reagan was doing what he did best:

A rare portrait of Reagan in his later years. On July 3, 1996, as part of his campaign for the presidency, Senator Robert Dole, together with his wife, Elizabeth, once Reagan's transportation secretary, visited the former president in his office in Century City, Los Angeles.

making us believe in a vision of America as a beacon of light in a world of darkness, as the home of an essentially brave and good people. "We will always remember," he said that long-ago day. "We will always be proud. We will always be prepared, so we may be always free." Freedom—from self-doubt, from the Soviet threat, from uneasiness about our national power and capacity to do great things—was Reagan's gift to his country.

He was ninety-three; for his devoted wife, Nancy, now eighty, her beloved husband's death ends a half-century love affair and a decade of anguishing illness and caregiving. She may find some comfort in the nation's outpouring of affection; few men in our history have been held in such warm regard. This week Reagan will receive a hero's farewell in Washington, lying in state in the rotunda of the Capitol followed by a funeral service at the National Cathedral. Then he will go home again, back across the nation, to be interred on the grounds of his presidential library in southern California's Simi Valley.

For Mrs. Reagan, it will be the final act of what she has called her husband's "long good-bye." For the rest of us, the passing of the fortieth president marks the close of one of the great American sagas: the rise and reign of the mysterious and elusive Ronald Reagan.

He fought the good fight for years. Toward the end, in the late 1990s, he could only remember the beginning. As Reagan's memory faded, the years seemed to fall away: the presidency, the governorship, Hollywood, sportscasting. Among his sharpest recollections was his youth in Illinois. In chats with guests in his Los Angeles office and in bits of conversation with his family at home in Bel Air, he would talk about learning to read newspapers on the front porch with his mother, about playing with his older brother, Neil, about setting off for the picture-perfect little campus of Eureka College. And there were his early days on the Rock River, where he swam in the summers and ice-skated in the winter. A picture of the river hung in his retirement office in Century City, and visitors would ask him about it. Again and again he would tell the story. "You know, that's where I used to be a lifeguard—I saved seventy-seven lives." There had been a log, he went on, where he carved a notch for every swimmer he rescued. "It was obviously an important part of his life, something he cherished," an aide recalled. "Being a lifeguard was ever-present in his memory." The image lingered when everything else was disappearing.

The lifeguard would grow up to seduce and shape America. When

Reagan became president in January 1981, the country was suffering from what his predecessor, Jimmy Carter, described as a "crisis of confidence." After triumph in World War II and the boom of the 1950s, postwar American optimism seemed to peak just before John F. Kennedy's assassination. After Dallas came Vietnam and Watergate. On Carter's watch inflation spiked, deficits soared, the Soviets invaded Afghanistan, and Islamic militants took fifty-two U.S. diplomats hostage in Iran. Serious people began to wonder whether the presidency was too big a job for any one man.

Then along came Reagan—nearly seventy, the emotionally distant son of an alcoholic Midwestern shoe salesman and a pious, theatrical mother. A former movie actor who gave his only critically acclaimed performance before Pearl Harbor, he was a sunny Californian who amiably ducked his head while talking tough on bureaucracy at home and communism abroad, pushing the nation's political conversation to the right.

In the White House, Reagan proved a maddeningly contradictory figure. An eloquent advocate of traditional values, he divorced his first wife and was often estranged from his children. A fierce advocate of balanced budgets, he never proposed one. A dedicated anticommunist, he reached out to the Soviet Union and helped end the cold war. An icon of button-down morality, he led an administration beleaguered by scandals. A man capable of nuanced thinking, he strongly believed in Armageddon.

He mangled facts; caricatured welfare recipients; opened his 1980 presidential campaign in Philadelphia, Mississippi, in the county where three civil-rights workers had been murdered for trying to overthrow Jim Crow; presided over a dark recession in 1982–83; seemed uncaring about the emerging HIV/AIDS crisis; and, in the Iran-contra scandal, came perilously close to—and may have committed—impeachable offenses.

Reagan, then, should have been as divisive a politician as Bill Clinton or George W. Bush—a man about whom the nation was closely and bitterly split. And while many people were consistently critical of Reagan, he still left office with a 63 percent approval rating. The roots of our own age's attack politics and ideological divisions lie in the Reagan years, yet the man himself seemed to dwell just above the arena, escaping widespread political enmity.

What was his secret? His personal gifts were enormous and helped smooth the rough edges of his rhetoric and his policies. Reagan was witty, eloquent, and bold. Wheeled into the operating room after being shot in the chest on March 30, 1981, the president looked up at the doctors and murmured, "Please tell me you're all Republicans." Coming to after the surgery, he whispered to Nancy, "Honey, I forgot to duck." At the Brandenburg Gate in 1987, he stood in the heart of divided Berlin and cried, "Mr. Gorbachev, open this gate. Mr. Gorbachev, tear down this wall." And eventually it was gone.

He felt more at home in the White House than any president since FDR. His uncommon public grace and mastery of television, in which he made his living long before he entered politics, largely redefined the role of chief executive. When he left the presidency in 1989, the Soviet Union was on its way to what Reagan had called "the ash heap of history." The American economy, though riven with deficits, hummed.

The audience loved him; even his foes conceded his charm. His political strength, however, came from more than theatrics. For all his tough-guy, "go ahead, make my day" rhetoric, Reagan was far more of a pragmatist than either his fans or his critics like to acknowledge. His words were stark, his deeds less so. In part this can be traced to one of the little-noticed eras of his long life: his years as president of the Screen Actors Guild in Hollywood, where, like all good union negotiators, he learned to make expansive, even excessive opening bids, knowing that in the end he would have to make a deal for less than what he had initially asked for. And so the Soviet Union was an "evil empire" in 1983. By 1986, Reagan, at Reykjavik, would consider eliminating all nuclear weapons if he could keep his beloved (yet impractical) Star Wars space shield. And by 1987 he had signed the first genuine arms-reduction treaty in cold-war history. The old SAG president had gotten the contract he wanted.

We are still living in the political world Reagan made. In his dedication to projecting power abroad and cutting taxes at home, President Bush often seems to be drawing more on the legend of the Gipper than on that of his own more mainstream, internationalist father. On the other side of the aisle, the Reagan movement—particularly his 49-state landslide over Walter Mondale in 1984—gave birth to the New Democrat centrism of Clinton: without the Reagan predicate, it is difficult to imagine that a Democratic president would have stood before Congress and declared that "the era of big government is over"—which Clinton did in 1996, the year he became the first two-term Democratic president since FDR.

The myth of the triumphant Gipper is a powerful one, but Reagan was more complex than his legend suggests. The man on horseback who rode to the rescue of a dispirited country started out as a shy child. The Manichean cold warrior was driven by a sentimental yearning for peace. The captivating charmer in public had little interest in the lives of other people, and no close friends.

The real Reagan was a romantic at heart. He saw the world as a cosmic struggle between good and evil, but he did not think it would all end in doom and destruction. Quite the opposite: He fervently held that everything would turn out for the best, and that he was destined to make it so. The boy who had been a lifeguard in the 1920s became the man who believed he would save the world from both totalitarianism and nuclear war. He thought he could, by personal persuasion, convince Moscow that it was on the wrong side of history. He would talk of taking a Soviet prime minister on a helicopter tour over the republic, pointing out the backyard swimming pools and second cars and boats in ordinary Americans' driveways. "If I can just get through to him about the difference between our two systems," Reagan would say wistfully, "I really think we could see big changes in the Soviet Union." There it all was, in that single bit of fantasy: a starring role, and a dream of saving the world.

He learned how to act, and dream, early on. In the winter of 1922, when Dutch was eleven years old, he found his father, Jack, passed out on the front porch. "He was drunk, dead to the world," Reagan recalled in his revealing 1965 memoir, *Where's the Rest of Me?* The boy's first instinct was to rearrange reality, to "pretend he wasn't there." Something else, though, began to stir in Reagan's heart on that cold evening. He realized it was time to take charge; later he understood this was his "first moment of accepting responsibility." So instead of stepping over Jack and slipping into bed, leaving the problem to his mother or his brother, Reagan saved his dad. "I bent over him, smelling the sharp odor of whiskey from the speakeasy," he recalled. "I got a fistful of his overcoat. Opening the door, I managed to drag him inside and get him to bed." And everything worked out, at least in Reagan's mind. "In a few days, he was the bluff, hearty man I knew and loved and will always remember."

In a few days. That must have been some bender, and though Reagan handled the crisis with the grace of a grown-up, he was still a little boy, one who could not help but be scared by the sight of his prostrate father. The drinking was a secret to be kept, a kind of trapdoor in the family's life: Reagan could never be sure when Jack would be engaging and hearty or when he would be flat on his back with snow in his hair.

Confronted by a chaotic childhood, Reagan sought refuge in a world of legendary exploits. This is not uncommon in the boyhoods of Great Men. Winston Churchill, long and painfully ignored by his parents, constructed an elaborate imaginary life as he grew up. The future British prime minister collected thousands of toy soldiers and devoured stories of great English military heroes; the young Reagan voraciously read Edgar Rice Burroughs's tales of adventure in outer space. Seeking order, he also joined his mother's church, the Disciples of Christ.

Young Reagan spent a lot of time with a childless elderly woman next door he called "Aunt Emma" who provided a 10-cent allowance, snacks, and solace. "The best part was that I was allowed to dream," he remembered. "Many the day I spent deep in a huge rocker in the mystic atmosphere of Aunt Emma's living room with its horsehair-stuffed gargoyles of furniture, its shawls and antimacassars, globes of glass over birds and flowers, books and strange odors." Like the adventure stories and the certitudes of church, Aunt Emma gave him sanctuary from the storm.

There were physical as well as psychological reasons for his dreaminess. Until high school he lived with a terrible, undiagnosed case of nearsightedness—so bad, in fact, that he had taught himself to act his way through most scenes. "I sat in the front row at school and still could not read the blackboard," Reagan said. "I bluffed my lessons and got fairly good marks, considering." Always competitive, he chose football over baseball and remembered the pleasure he found in exerting force. On the gridiron there "was no invisible little ball—just another guy to grab or knock down, and it didn't matter if his face was blurred." Then one day in the car, bothered that Neil could read the road signs and he could not, Reagan tried his mother's glasses. "Putting them on, I suddenly saw a glorious, sharply outlined world jump into focus and shouted with delight," he said. "I was astounded to find out trees had sharply defined separate leaves; houses had a definite texture and hills really made a clear silhouette against the sky." But he had dwelled for a long time in his own universe, where his thoughts and feelings were the only crisply defined realities; everything outside himself—parents, teachers, friends—had been shrouded and gauzy. "Although he loves people," Nancy Davis Reagan would say decades later, "he often seems remote, and he doesn't let anybody get too close. There's a wall around him. He lets me come closer than anyone else, but there are times when even I feel that barrier."

Yet Reagan was not an angry man. Rather than rail against life's unfairness, he would recast unpleasant truths in a more flattering light. His mother had taught him how. A devout woman, Nelle must have been severely disappointed in her alcoholic husband, but she tried her best to put a cheerful face on the darkest of things, beginning with Jack's addiction. "Like my mother, I came to dread those days when he'd take the first drink," Reagan recalled. "Although he wasn't the kind of alcoholic who was abusive to his wife or children, he could be pretty surly, and my brother and I heard a lot of cursing when Mother went after him for his drinking." In front of the boys, though, Nelle insisted that they forgive their father. "Nelle always looked for and found the goodness in people," Reagan said. Put another way, she made the best of the worst, essentially acting her way through difficult situations. Some would call that denial; others, stoicism. Whatever it was, her son inherited it.

Though Reagan came from nowhere, with no significant connections in the greater world, there was a kind of momentum in his life. "Our family didn't exactly come from the wrong side of the tracks," he recalled, "but we were certainly always within sound of the train whistles." To get ahead he mastered his immediate universe, using the mechanics of popularity available to public-high-school and small-college kids in twentieth-century America. He played football, cut a dashing figure at the lifeguard stand during the summers, pledged a good fraternity at Eureka College, found a good job at a radio station in the worst period of the Depression, and stumbled into a screen test for Warner Bros. while he was covering the Cubs' spring training in southern California.

Through it all, he hit his marks. The role of the theater in his life was a gift from his mother, an organizer of readings and performances in Illinois. She urged him to declaim a speech one night before the local crowd, but the shy Dutch was reluctant. Another streak in his character—his competitive-

ABOVE: In 1944 Ronald Reagan was a captain in the United States Army Air Force. Reagan and his wife, Jane Wyman, share the stage in this Hollywood publicity shot with their three-year-old-daughter, Maureen.

OPPOSITE: Reagan and Diana Lynn—with chimpanzee—in a scene from the 1951 movie *Bedtime for Bonzo*.

ness—pushed him forward. "My brother had already given several and been a hit," Reagan said. So he would do it too. "Summoning up my courage, I walked up to the stage that night, cleared my throat, and made my theatrical debut," he recalled. "I don't remember what I said, but I'll never forget the response: people laughed and applauded."

Suddenly a new world opened before him. Onstage, Jack's drinking didn't matter, and his shyness, born of nearsightedness and his family's frequent moves, melted away in the warmth of the audience's approval. "That was a new experience for me and I liked it," Reagan said. "For a kid suffering childhood pangs of insecurity, the applause was music." He would spend the rest of his long life seeking to hear just those notes, first in Hollywood and then from Orange County to Red Square.

In Hollywood he became a midlevel star after an apprenticeship in the Bs, where he found fame playing heroic Secret Service Agent Brass Bancroft in a series of movies. (The agent who shoved President Reagan into his car and saved his life during the assassination attempt in 1981, Jerry Parr, had been a member of the Junior Brass Bancroft Society.) "So much of our profession is taken up with pretending, with the interpretation of never-never roles, that an actor must spend at least half his waking hours in fantasy, in rehearsal or shooting," Reagan once said. He found comfort in that.

Reagan was not a bad screen actor, just an ordinary one, and he was prideful about his movie career. Years later he would admit to his biographer Lou Cannon that criticism of his film performances (which ran to jokes about *Bedtime for Bonzo*, a 1951 comedy) "touched an exposed nerve."

In the late 1930s and the 1940s, the movie world gave Reagan a home in a company town, a very good living and, in 1940, a wife, Jane Wyman. Reagan's heart had already been broken once. His high school love, Margaret Cleaver, had thrown him over for a Foreign Service officer, mailing back Reagan's fraternity pin and engagement ring. "Like my mother," he recalled, "she was short, pretty, auburn haired, and intelligent." Though crushed, Reagan characteristically did not dwell on the loss. "Something inside me suggested that things would work out all right," he said. Still, there was a vacuum. "Margaret's decision shattered me, not so much, I think, because she no longer loved me, but because I no longer had anyone to love."

Wyman filled that void. It was not an ordinary boy-meets-girl story: the marriage was in part a product of the publicity culture of Hollywood. They met filming *Brother Rat*, and the gossip columnist Louella Parsons nurtured the relationship. They had a daughter, Maureen, in 1941, and adopted a son, Michael, after Reagan's service in the moviemaking arm of the military in Culver City. Later they lost a child, named Christine, at the same time that Reagan was battling a potentially deadly case of viral pneumonia. A hospitalized Reagan thought he was going to die. "I don't know what time of night it was when I told the nurse I was too tired to breathe anymore," he recalled, but she coached him through a spiking fever.

The usual version of the story of the divorce has Wyman's career taking off while Reagan's sputtered and he grew more interested in politics and his job as president of the Screen Actors Guild. Neither Reagan nor Wyman ever publicly broke a dignified, decades-long silence about the end of their marriage. Reagan claimed to be oblivious to whatever difficulties there were. He returned to California from testifying before Congressman Richard Nixon's House Un-American Activities Committee to find Wyman seeking divorce. As with Margaret Cleaver, he was wounded but moved on. He always did.

What drove him, what gave him the serenity and sense of security to force himself forward through life's storms with a smile and a wave? Partly it was what he had absorbed in Aunt Emma's parlor and on the porch with Nelle and on the river: that he was destined to become one of the heroes he loved to read about, a hero for whom everything would work out. He went from strength to strength. Reagan had an unreliable father but succeeded in high school and college. He entered the wider world in the depths of the Depression but found jobs with comparative ease. He lost two loves but in 1952 married Nancy Davis, a woman who became his anchor. His movie career sputtered, but he made a living in television. When the TV contract went away, politics beckoned. Who, experiencing such a life, wouldn't be confident of the basic goodness of the universe?

He met Nancy on a blind date: he loved her laugh. To him she represented order, love, stability—and forward movement. "If Ronnie had married Nancy the first time," James Stewart once remarked, "he would have won an Academy Award." But by the time of their wedding (their daughter, Patti, was born seven months later; Ron would follow in 1958), Reagan's movie career was stalled. He then spent eight years as a genial visitor in Americans' living rooms every Sunday night as the host of *General Electric Theater*. Progress put him out of a job: *Bonanza*, a color Western, swamped his black-and-white show in 1962. For the first time since he had stepped in front of his mother's theatrical group as a child, Reagan was looking for a role.

He found one in politics. By his own account he had idolized FDR during the thirties, and he had campaigned for Harry Truman. But anticommunism, high taxes, and, while he was working for GE, worries about government regulation pushed him to the right. In October 1964 Barry Goldwater's presidential campaign was going nowhere, and the national Republican Party asked Reagan to give a half-hour national address (to devotees it is known simply as The Speech). Viewed today, forty years later, he seems so young, so crisp, so sure of himself and his beliefs. He would not change much in the ensuing twenty-five years of his public life. Lyndon Johnson crushed Goldwater, but in 1966 a group of California moneymen bankrolled a Reagan campaign for governor against the formidable Democratic incumbent, Edmund (Pat) Brown.

Brown was the first politician to make a mistake many others would repeat: He underestimated Reagan. The Gipper—he could not resist adopting his screen persona from *Knute Rockne, All American*—was an emblem and an architect of a new force in American politics: the rise of the suburban conservatives. Elected governor in 1966, he was the fresh face of conservatism; a 1967 *Newsweek* cover asked, REAGAN: A RISING STAR IN THE WEST?

The answer was an emphatic yes. The next year he nearly stopped Nixon's nomination in Miami after less than two years as governor. He would spend the next few years honing his message and building toward another run for the White House. Like many political coalitions, Reagan's was eclectic. He brought together country-club Republicans interested in lower taxes, evangelical Christians, and traditional Democrats disaffected by the chaos of the 1960s, and especially in the South he would inherit the fruits of Nixon's "Southern strategy" of coded racial appeals.

A 1967 photograph of Ronald and Nancy Reagan, with their son Ron and daughter Patti.

When Reagan went to Sacramento, he was asked what he planned to do. "I don't know," he quipped. "I've never played a governor." But he did know. He was crisp in execution and deft at communication. Willie Brown, the liberal Democratic legislator known as the Ayatollah for his heavy-handed ways in Sacramento, recalled that Reagan was the only governor he ever worked with who got things done on time. Gerald Ford, whom Reagan would challenge for the Republican presidential nomination in 1976, remembered that Reagan was the man in the room after a meeting who could find the perfect phrase for a press release.

Reagan was not all style; he represented a real shift in American politics, but both in California and later in Washington his revolutions were never quite as dramatic as his followers hoped or his foes feared. Neither state nor federal governments actually shrank on Reagan's watch, and he never genuinely pushed for the more controversial dreams of his hard-right cultural base. He talked about school prayer and curbing abortion rights, but he never did much more than that.

By 1976 he was tired of waiting his turn and was worried that President Ford was being too open to the Soviets. In a closely fought primary season, Ford won, but he needed Reagan to appeal to conservatives, particularly conservative Christians, who were intrigued by the born-again Jimmy Carter. Reagan, however, was reluctant to campaign for the president. Even years later Ford loyalists could recount the precise counties where a Reagan swing in the fall of 1976 would have helped, particularly in conservative pockets of key border states.

For Reagan the story seemed over. He was getting old—he would be sixty-nine in 1980—and the oldest president in history, Dwight Eisenhower, had retired at that age. But Reagan was just getting started.

The victory over Carter in '80 was far from foreordained. Reagan lost the Iowa caucuses to George Bush but recovered; until October 28, a week before the general election, Reagan and Carter were running close together in the polls. Then came Cleveland. In their single debate, Reagan delivered devastating blows. The first was shaking his head and saying, more in sorrow than in anger, "There you go again" when Carter accused him of wanting to cut Medicare (Reagan did, but the theatrical gesture was what voters remembered, not the details). Then, in his closing statement, Reagan posed two simple questions: "Are you better off than you were four years ago? Is America as respected throughout the world as it was?" For many Americans, troubled by inflation, interest rates, and the Iranian hostage crisis, the answer was no, and the ground shifted to Reagan in that final week. He won in a landslide.

Reagan was right at home in the White House. "My husband loved being president," Nancy said. "He enjoyed it, all of it—the decision making, the responsibilities, the negotiating, as well as the ceremonies, the public appearances and the meetings."

He invented stories and then believed them. He thought trees produced pollution, confusing carbon dioxide with carbon monoxide. Welfare was bad because of a mysterious Chicago "welfare queen" who drove a Cadillac

while on relief. And on and on. His fictions were real to him, which was both touching and somewhat terrifying. According to Reagan biographer Lou Cannon, Colin Powell, then the national security advisor, used to cringe when Reagan would trot out his "little green men" theory, the idea being that extraterrestrial life might one day attack us and force the nations of the globe to get along. A fine sentiment, if more than a little disconcerting coming from a president with control of the nuclear codes.

There were many derelictions and failures on the home front. Reagan could not control spending enough to balance the budget after he cut taxes, leaving a deficit of $152.5 billion when he left office; on his watch the national debt nearly tripled. When the reckoning came—at an Andrews Air Force Base summit in the hot summer of 1990 between President Bush and Democratic congressional leaders—Reagan was long gone, in retirement. It was Bush, then, who had to raise taxes, breaking a 1988 pledge and alienating the right. What was good for the country—

many economists credit the 1990 budget deal with setting the stage for the boom of the Clinton years—was bad for Bush, but Reagan had created the problem.

Though Reagan was a soft touch for individual stories of pain or misfortune, the poor fared badly in the 1980s, and too many Americans of color felt left out. Seemingly oblivious, the president prided himself on his belief that he was without prejudice, often telling an anecdote about how his father would refuse to stay in a hotel that refused to accept Jews or blacks. But that story did not translate into compassion for those left out of the American Dream Reagan so cherished. In truth, he was probably as conflicted as many white Americans on questions of race and generosity. Because he did not hate, he could not see how his ambivalence (about preferences, about spending on the poor, about police misconduct or homelessness) could appear to others as indifference—or, worse, outright hostility. There is no question, however, that it did appear precisely that way to millions of Americans, and Reagan of all people should have known that appearances can be much the same as reality. He should have done better by those on the fringes of his fabled "shining city on a hill." For them, stirring words were not enough.

In what was perhaps the most brilliant critique of Reagan in real time, the then New York governor, Mario Cuomo, turned this favorite Reagan image of the shining city against the president. "The hard truth is that not everyone is sharing in this city's splendor and glory," Cuomo said in his keynote address to the 1984 Democratic National Convention. "A shining city is perhaps all the president sees from the portico of the White House and the veranda of his ranch, where everyone seems to be doing well. But there's another city; there's another part to the shining city; the part where some people can't pay their mortgages and most young people can't afford one, where students can't afford the education they need and middle-class parents watch the dreams they hold for their children evaporate." A devastating indictment, and one that had much truth in it. For many, the Gipper's America was a movie in which they had no part.

Reagan came to power as a consummate cold warrior. Skeptical of the Nixon-Ford era of détente with the Soviets and eager to build mighty armies, including a defensive missile shield in outer space, he wanted to send Moscow an unmistakable message that accommodation was not possible. The hawks were happy, the doves apoplectic.

Both camps should have watched Reagan with a colder eye, for he was playing a complicated game. In 1983—the same year he called the Soviet Union an "evil empire"—the president asked Secretary of State George Shultz to bring Soviet ambassador Anatoly Dobrynin by for a secret chat, opening a quiet channel that helped lead to the thaw of the second term. There is an ongoing debate over what brought the Soviet Union to its knees. Reagan's admirers believe it was his unflinching rhetoric and unrelenting military buildup; his critics argue that the Soviets were intrinsically weak and would have imploded even if Carter had been reelected in 1980, consigning Reagan to an early retirement in California.

The truth probably lies somewhere in between. There were many forces at work in what President Kennedy called the "long twilight struggle" between communism and democratic capitalism, but Reagan's dual strategy of articulating a stark vision—including insisting on developing the Strategic Defense Initiative, or Star Wars—and of conducting steady diplomacy almost certainly accelerated the fall of Soviet totalitarianism. His personal connection to Mikhail Gorbachev was important to

Using a giant replica of a tax form as a prop, President Reagan promotes his latest income tax reform proposal, in Bloomfield, New Jersey, June 13, 1985.

Reagan and helped make the disarmament talks of the mid-1980s possible and productive. At first skeptical of the old actor, the Soviet reformer came to appreciate him.

Still, Reagan's older cold-war instincts helped bring on the defining scandal of his presidency, the Iran-contra affair. In violation of the law, the Reagan administration secretly used money raised from the sale of weapons to Iran to fund the Nicaraguan contras who were leading an anti-Marxist-Leninist insurgency.

What did Reagan know? Perhaps little; specifics were never his strong suit. "From our first meeting," Gorbachev recalled, "I had noticed President Reagan's dislike for detail."

The president and first lady boarding the presidential helicopter on the South Lawn of the White House prior to leaving for a Camp David visit with Margaret Thatcher, November 14, 1986.

But Reagan created the climate in which his White House broke the law, prompting a constitutional crisis over executive power. Reagan will answer to history for Iran-contra. His motives may have been admirable, but his means were not.

It was a bleak time. When he called former Tennessee senator Howard Baker to offer him the job of White House chief of staff in the wake of the scandal, Baker's then wife, Joy, answered the telephone. "Howard's not here, Mr. President," she said. "He's taken the grandchildren to the zoo." Without missing a beat, Reagan replied: "Wait till he sees the zoo I've got in mind for him."

Baker was replacing Donald Regan, and Regan—who was essentially fired by Nancy Reagan—got his revenge. In a book published when the Reagans were still in the White House, Regan wrote that the first lady regularly consulted a San Francisco astrologer, Joan Quigley, to guide the president's schedule. (Quigley had been recommended to Nancy by Merv Griffin.) The defense that Nancy had turned to the stars for protection only after the 1981 assassination attempt did not help much. It was not the kind of story an elderly president who had spent his life in Hollywood and was now immersed in scandal and facing questions about his fitness for office needed just then (or ever). There was so much speculation about Reagan's health and state of mind after Iran-contra broke at Thanksgiving 1986, Washington journalists Jane Mayer and Doyle McManus later reported, that an incoming Baker aide, James Cannon, was privately asked to research the 25th Amendment's provisions for dealing with an incapacitated president.

As always, though, Reagan defied expectations and rolled on. The breakthroughs with Gorbachev and a strong economy nudged his approval numbers back up as 1988 approached. Never close to George Bush—Ford had been Reagan's first choice for a running mate in 1980—the president seemed unenthusiastic about his loyal veep's campaign for the top job in the Republican primaries. Four years later, in 1992, as Bush was under attack from conservatives for raising taxes and appearing to tack too far to the center, a rumor began to circulate in true-believer circles. According to the memoirs of speechwriter John Podhoretz, Reagan is supposed to have mused aloud: "I guess I really effed it up in 1980"—by choosing Bush.

Not entirely convincingly, Reagan long claimed to want to go home to the ranch and to private life. In the end, though, the pleasures of retirement would be tragically brief. At the 1992 Republican National Convention he seemed tired, shushing the crowd with uncharacteristic weariness. The performance was a world away from his buoyant 1980 acceptance speech, where he had wittily controlled the cheers by quipping: "We're using up prime time." Now, a dozen years later, he struck many for the first time as a truly

Reagan and Gorbachev talking outside the White House prior to signing the Intermediate Nuclear Forces (INF) Treaty, December 8, 1987.

old man. He grew more forgetful. During an awkward after-dinner scene with Queen Elizabeth II aboard the royal yacht *Britannia* in 1991, captured by a BBC documentary crew, Reagan was entirely focused on getting a cup of decaffeinated coffee. There was shuffling, uncertainty, missed cues. "Well, we do try," the queen said. Nancy looked nervous, on edge, trying to get through. A 1994 appearance in Washington sealed it: a campaign speech was stilted. Something was wrong.

It was Alzheimer's. On November 5, 1994, Reagan took up a black pen and said good-bye to the nation. As usual, it was a fluid, virtuoso performance, the Gipper at the pinnacle of his powers, leaving a permanent testament of his essential grace. "When the Lord calls me home, whenever that may be, I will leave with the greatest love for this country of ours and eternal optimism for its future," Reagan wrote. "I now begin the journey that

will lead me into the sunset of my life. I know that for America there will always be a bright dawn ahead. Thank you, my friends. May God always bless you."

He retreated to the house on St. Cloud Drive in Bel Air. For a time he went to the office, took strolls on the Santa Monica pier, hit golf balls. Later those things became impossible. At home he still responded to red, whether his daughter Maureen's bright fingernails or a cheery birthday sweater. Reagan's strength—his primal will to live—was amazing. He survived year after year after year, recovered from a broken hip, endured and endured. His body fought for life long after his mind had honorably surrendered to disease.

All his life he was a dreamer, and his imagination had sustained him through the decades in ways big and small. In a remarkable letter written from the Sherry-Netherland Hotel at the corner of 59th Street and Fifth Avenue in Manhattan on a July day in the 1950s, Reagan displayed his gift for softening the rough edges of life with visions of better things. He was lonely, in the city for an acting job, and had to eat alone. Afterward, back at the hotel, he wrote Nancy about the evening he wished he'd had—with her.

"Eight million people in this pigeon crap encrusted metropolis and suddenly I realized I was alone with my thoughts and they smelled sulphurous," he wrote her. "Time was not a healer. When dinnertime finally arrived I walked down to '21,' where I ate in lonely splendor. It was at this point with self-pity coming up fast on the rail that you joined me. Yes, you and I had Roast Beef . . . Wanting only half a bottle of wine we were somewhat restricted in choice but we politely resisted the 'huxtering' of the wine steward . . . and settled for a '47 'Pichon Longueville.' It was tasty, wasn't it?"

The meal done, Reagan's imagination kept the movie going. "We walked back in the twilight and I guess I hadn't ought to put us on paper from there on," he continued. "Let's just say I didn't know my lines this morning. Tonight I think we'll eat at the hotel and you've got to promise to let me study—at least for a little while. I suppose some people would find it unusual that you and I can so easily span three thousand miles but in truth it comes very naturally. Man can't live without a heart and you are my heart, by far the nicest thing about me and so very necessary. There would be no life without you nor would I want any."

As she has been for more than fifty years, Nancy will be by his side this week. After the ceremonies in Washington, Reagan will be laid to rest in California on a hill near a relic of the Berlin Wall, the closing chapter in a long story that began in a tiny house in Illinois in the winter of 1911. His grave looks out toward the Pacific, where the sun sets on America every evening. It is still light there, on the edge of the continent, when darkness has fallen across the rest of the nation. How like Reagan: soaking up the last possible ray of sun, savoring the day to the very end.

OPPOSITE: Ronald Reagan's presidential library in Simi Valley, California, was dedicated in November, 1991. Reagan speaks at the ceremony.

BELOW: Five U.S. presidents attended the dedication ceremony for the presidential library. From the left: incumbent and number 41, George H. W. Bush; number 40, Ronald Reagan; number 39, Jimmy Carter; number 38, Gerald Ford; and number 37, Richard Nixon.

RIGHT: During Ronald Reagan's eightieth birthday celebrations, the president's long-time staunch ally, former British prime minister Margaret Thatcher visits the former president at the site of his presidential library in Simi Valley, California. The two former leaders pose in front of a section of the demolished Berlin Wall donated to the library.

Los Angeles Times, June 9, 2004

FAREWELL TO A PRESIDENT

by Steve Chawkins

———

The admirers just kept coming.

By night's end Tuesday, more than 105,000 had trooped solemnly by Ronald Reagan's flag-draped casket at his presidential library near Simi Valley.

Most were ferried by bus from nearby Moorpark College, where they waited in line for as long as seven hours.

While plans for the viewing were years in the making, nobody anticipated a crush of visitors so overwhelming that even before dawn on Tuesday, traffic was halted for hours on the Ronald Reagan Freeway.

At the Reagan home in Bel Air, where the former president died Saturday at age ninety-three, Nancy Reagan said she was stunned by the turnout, said Joanne Drake, chief of staff at Reagan's office.

"It is unbelievable what I am seeing on TV," Drake quoted the former first lady as saying. "The outpouring of love for my husband is incredible."

So many visitors kept streaming to the presidential library that officials delayed the end of viewing hours from 6 P.M. to 11 P.M.

On Tuesday afternoon, Massachusetts senator John F. Kerry, the presumptive Democratic presidential candidate, paid his respects with a moment of silence beside the casket. He made the sign of the cross and bowed his head.

Kerry was in Los Angeles for his daughter's graduation from the American Film Institute. Both he and President Bush will attend the late president's funeral at the National Cathedral in Washington, D.C., on Friday. After the services, the body will be returned to the library grounds for burial.

While Kerry's entourage glided up the hill in a motorcade, a seemingly endless caravan of buses hauled parents with their

Nancy Reagan and her children, Ron Reagan and Patti Davis, look at the tributes left at the funeral home in Santa Monica, California, where the former president's body has been lying before it is moved to the presidential library, June 7, 2004.

young children, elderly people with canes and wheelchairs, old soldiers bidding farewell to their former commander in chief, legions of people who fondly recalled the fortieth president's wide-open face and sunny wit.

"I feel blessed to be here," said Shirley Venus Wake, a fifty-one-year-old Pasadena secretary. "I became a Republican because of him. Everything was just great then."

Even critics of Reagan's administration were moved by what they saw at his library.

"I spent a decade blaming him for things because I'm a union person," said Jeanne Edwards, a Thousand Oaks mother who was persuaded to visit by her eighteen-year-old daughter, Kira. "I knew at the time I didn't like his policies, but you couldn't not like him as a person."

The tide of well-wishers swelled Monday night and Tuesday morning. From the hilltop library, visitors gazing across the valley could see a chain of red lights as motorists inched along. Before dawn on Tuesday, a few frustrated drivers left their

Paying respects. As Ronald Reagan's casket lies at his presidential library in Simi Valley prior to its journey to Washington, D.C., his family gathers. From the left are Ronald Prescott Reagan, Reverend Michael Wenning, Nancy Reagan, Patti Davis, and Michael Reagan and his daughter Ashley.

cars on the freeway shoulder and trudged miles to Moorpark College, where they would wait some more.

At the library turnoff on Olsen Road, police officers staffed a checkpoint beside a makeshift shrine. An electric highway sign read: "Road Closed. Flower Drop Only."

Moments after viewing Reagan's casket, Andrea Mejia said she was exhausted.

"I loved him," the Sunland woman said. "I prayed for him. If it was hours ago, I would have cried. But it's 3 A.M. and we stood in line for seven hours. We're physically and emotionally drained."

Her daughter, graduate student Jacobi Lynn Mejia, said she was mentally preserving "every detail, every image." That way, she could pass a piece of history to her family's next generation—just like her great-great-aunt who told of Abraham Lincoln's funeral train passing slowly through her small Ohio town.

For many, their hours in Ventura County carried a similar weight.

A few older men wore suits and a few women wore dresses, but most of the visitors looked as informal as any group of Californians on a day off. As they slowly filed past the casket on its rectangle of blue carpet, they were silent. Here, a woman brushed away a tear; there, a gray-haired man drew himself up and offered a crisp military salute.

Six members of a military honor guard stood at attention beside the bier, their eyes never flickering. They were a stately grace note to memories of Reagan as a down-home hero.

"He was just so human," said Linda Martins, a mortgage company employee from Simi Valley. "He was never afraid to show his feelings. You knew just where he stood."

Toting a sketch pad, Martins had passed the time during her long wait by drawing a rose, an angel, an eagle.

"I wish I could have drawn a horse and left it on his casket," she said. "How else would a cowboy ride off with God?"

Some of the visitors praised Reagan for specific accomplishments while he was in office.

Wei Chao, a physician from Hong Kong, said he wanted to pay his respects to the president who had signed the joint communiqué of August

17, 1982—a pact in which the United States agreed to limit arms sales to Taiwan.

"That took wisdom and courage," he said. "We are in the presence of greatness."

Marvin Amaya of North Hollywood said he was paying tribute to Reagan "on behalf of my family."

"The amnesty law he signed in 1986 allowed me to adjust my immigration status and attend college," said Amaya, who originally is from El Salvador.

Many couples endured the lengthy wait to offer their children the memory of a lifetime.

Simi Valley resident Chris Cook and his wife, Tracy, brought their nine-year-old son, Daniel.

Tracy said the family's Christmas card in 2001 was a shot of them in front of the chunk of the Berlin Wall that is the centerpiece of the library grounds. When they sent out that card, they decided they would bring Daniel with them to Reagan's viewing when the time came.

"We wanted to be a part of it," Tracy said. "We figured this is more a day of education than he'd ever get in a day of school."

Times *staff writers Amanda Covarrubias, Matea Gold, Gregory W. Griggs, and Regine Labossiere contributed to this report.*

The Philadelphia Inquirer, June 11, 2004

For Thousands in Line, Personal Farewells

by Ron Hutcheson,
Inquirer *Washington Bureau*

Tens of thousands of Americans and foreign visitors from all walks of life filed past the casket of Ronald Reagan yesterday, pausing to pay their respects to the nation's fortieth president.

World leaders including his long-ago Soviet rival Mikhail S. Gorbachev were among those who gazed upon his casket in hushed contemplation in the Capitol Rotunda. President Bush, back from his meeting with world leaders in Georgia, briefly paid respects in advance of his eulogy at the national funeral today at Washington National Cathedral.

Across from the White House, Nancy Reagan received a stream of visitors drawn from a list of the powerful, then and now.

As many as 200,000 people were expected to have paid their respects inside the Rotunda by the end of the round-the-clock vigil early this morning.

Yesterday, mourners found different ways to pay tribute as they circled a funeral platform that was hastily built in 1865 to hold Abraham Lincoln's casket.

Aging veterans and young soldiers in uniform snapped off salutes. Some Reagan admirers blinked back tears. Others placed their hands over their hearts or made the sign of the cross. Most simply stared at the coffin or shifted their gaze from the casket to the soaring dome 180 feet overhead, where a painting from 1865 shows George Washington ascended to heaven.

"It was worth three hours standing in line sweating," said David Judd of Baltimore, a retired lawyer who described himself as "a Democrat who respects the man."

David Christensen of Livonia, Michigan, drove to Washington with his wife, Laura, and twin four-year-old daughters to pay his respects. Christensen, forty-eight, said he once received a D college paper for defending Reagan's view that tax cuts for the wealthy ultimately would benefit Americans at all income levels.

"I've always believed in him," Christensen said.

The Capitol sergeant at arms office, which oversees security in the building, estimated 30,000 people had viewed the casket in the first ten hours of Reagan's lying in state. The casket was to be on public view for more than thirty hours.

Throughout the day, average citizens were joined from time to time by prominent figures. Gorbachev, Senator Edward M. Kennedy (D., Mass.), former senator Bob Dole (R., Kan.), Senator John McCain (R., Ariz.), and a

The caisson carrying the body of former President Reagan moves toward the U.S. Capitol in Washington, D.C., June 9, 2004.

ABOVE: As part of the procession, a riderless horse with an empty pair of the president's boots facing backward in the stirrups symbolizing a fallen warrior is walked behind the carriage carrying the former president's body to the Capitol.

RIGHT: The casket of former President Reagan lies in state in the Capitol Rotunda in Washington, D.C., where thousands stand in line for hours to pay tribute.

host of other lawmakers from both parties were among those who walked around the casket.

Gorbachev, who was permitted inside the velvet ropes surrounding the bier, placed his hand on the American flag covering the casket and nodded toward the body of the man who had called the Soviet Union the evil empire before he forged a series of agreements with Gorbachev.

After wrapping up an international summit in Sea Island, Georgia, Bush headed back to Washington to visit the Rotunda and express condolences to Nancy Reagan, who was offered the use of Blair House, the government guest residence across Pennsylvania Avenue from the White House.

The president laid both hands on Reagan's casket.

"Ronald Reagan was a great man, a historic leader, and a national treasure," Bush said before leaving Georgia. The president said he intended to deliver the thanks of a "grateful nation" at today's service.

Former British prime minister Margaret Thatcher was the first to see Nancy Reagan at Blair House. "To Ronnie," Thatcher wrote in the condolence book. "Well done, thou good and faithful servant."

Reagan and Thatcher shared a worldview, conservative politics, and enduring mutual affection.

Former Canadian prime minister Brian Mulroney, who shared an Irish ancestry with Reagan, also visited the former first lady, with his wife, Mila. "For Ron with affection, admiration, and respect," the Mulroneys wrote. "The Gipper always came through!"

Gorbachev visited, too, and wrote in the condolence book in Russian: "I convey my deep feelings of condolence to dear Nancy and the whole family."

Former secretary of state George Shultz and former chief of staff Howard Baker were among the onetime Reagan aides who went to Blair House.

Thatcher and Mulroney are joining Bush and his father, former president George H. W. Bush, today in eulogizing Reagan to close the curtain on the elaborate state funeral.

The other living former presidents are also expected: Gerald R. Ford, Jimmy Carter, and Bill Clinton.

The 11:30 A.M. memorial service will cap forty-four hours of state-funeral ceremonies that gave thousands of Americans a chance to say good-bye. Reagan, who died at his California home Saturday at age ninety-three, will be buried at sunset today at his presidential library in Simi Valley, California.

Today's funeral will be restricted to the powerful, the prominent, and the well-connected, but yesterday was a time for people such as Michael Moyer of Carlisle, Pennsylvania, to show their gratitude and affection for the former president.

After reporting for work at a Federal Express shipping center at 3:00 A.M. yesterday, Moyer, sixty-two, got off early to catch a 7:30 A.M. bus to the nation's capital.

"It's just special to be here and show our appreciation," Moyer said outside the Capitol, wearing a hat fashioned from a newspaper as protection against the sun. "He did so much to unite the nation."

Nancy Reagan kisses her husband's casket as it lies in the Capitol Rotunda, June 11, 2004. President Reagan's remains are about to be taken to California for burial later in the day.

Los Angeles Times, June 12, 2004

FAREWELL TO A PRESIDENT

by Faye Fiore, Vicki Kemper, and Daryl Kelley, Times Staff Writers

---

Ronald Wilson Reagan, the nation's fortieth president, was buried on a golden Southern California hilltop Friday, after a funeral in Washington National Cathedral attended by hundreds of world leaders, past and present.

The ceremonies ended a week of mourning and majesty that honored the uniquely American figure who was credited with hastening the end of the cold war. Reagan died June 5 at ninety-three.

A presidential jet delivered his body to California, where the former statesman and showman was laid to rest in a horseshoe-shaped burial site at the Ronald Reagan Presidential Library—shaded by seven oak trees and overlooking a panoramic farm valley, with the Pacific Ocean beyond.

The day began in the gray mist of a Washington drizzle and ended in the glow of a California sunset. Formal tributes in the nation's capital gave way to the more intimate embrace of the Santa Susana Mountains and the tender memories of the children who loved him.

Michael Reagan spoke of his father's gift of Christian faith and his advice on how to have a long and happy marriage: "You'll never get in trouble if you say 'I love you' at least once a day."

Patti Davis recounted how the man who would be president taught his daughter about death by helping her bury her goldfish.

And Ronald Prescott Reagan talked about his father's optimism, his struggle with Alzheimer's disease, and his last trip home: "In his final letter to the American people, Dad wrote: 'I now

TOP: President George W. Bush speaks during the funeral service in the National Cathedral in Washington, June 11, 2004.

BOTTOM: With key figures from the lifetime of Ronald Reagan looking on, a military honor guard carries the casket of the former president after funeral services at the National Cathedral in Washington, D.C., have concluded.

begin the journey that will lead me into the sunset of my life.' This evening, he has arrived."

Luminaries and laymen on both coasts searched Friday for ways to honor the son of a Midwestern shoe salesman who had risen to Hollywood celebrity, the California governorship, and a presidency that spawned a conservative era in American politics.

"Ronald Reagan belongs to the ages now, but we preferred it when he belonged to us," President Bush said during an interfaith service in the majestic cathedral, where about 3,500 people gathered in one of the greatest assemblages of power and influence the capital had seen in decades. "When the sun sets tonight off the coast of California and we lay to rest our fortieth president, a great American story will close."

It was a ceremony of solemn music and soaring tribute. Bush's voice cracked once; his father, President George H. W. Bush, fought back tears. But for Nancy Reagan, eighty-two, her husband's companion and fierce protector throughout public life, it was a day spent letting go.

"There was only one person he said could make him lonely by just leaving the room," President Bush said in one of several nods to the former first lady, who looked frail and spent as she persevered through the seventh straight day of public mourning. "America honors you, Nancy, for the loyalty and love you gave this man on a wonderful journey."

On his last day, in his last moments, Reagan himself had paid mute tribute to his beloved wife. In her graveside eulogy at the presidential library, Davis described her father's end: "He opened his eyes, eyes that had not opened for many, many days, and looked at my mother. He showed us that neither disease nor death can conquer love."

Only hours before the Washington service began, the public viewing of the casket—draped in the flag that flew over the Capitol the day Reagan was inaugurated in 1981—came to an end in the Rotunda of the U.S. Capitol. An estimated 104,000 people had filed past in thirty-six hours.

Friday morning before leaving Blair House, the official residence of White House guests, Mrs. Reagan met with the personal staff from her own White House days—including her maid, ushers, pastry chef, gardener, and the president's valet.

Shortly afterward, Mrs. Reagan rode to the Capitol, where she stood in the ornate Rotunda, alone at her husband's side. She rubbed her hands over the cloth and spoke words no one could hear. Then she bent to kiss the coffin, reached for the arm of her military escort, hesitated, and turned back for one final pat.

Three World War II–vintage howitzers cracked a 21-gun salute before nine military pallbearers ferried the casket to a waiting hearse for the 4½-mile processional to the cathedral. Mrs. Reagan, her face strained but focused, watched until the coffin slid safely into the hearse, a black umbrella held by a gloved military attendant shielding her from the rain.

Outside the cathedral, the mahogany coffin—said to be larger and more ornate than any used for former presidents—glided from the back of the hearse to a chorus of "Hail to the Chief," a tune Reagan loved even more than most. He saluted crisply whenever he heard it.

The ninety-minute service was timed to the second. At 11:18, the church fell silent. The coffin passed through the door at precisely 11:30. After Mrs. Reagan was escorted down the aisle, President Bush stood to meet her and clasp her hand. She was seated beside her children and Michael Reagan, the son of the former president and his first wife, actress Jane Wyman.

Around them were the four living ex-presidents and their wives, all nine Supreme Court justices, cabinet secretaries past and present, virtually the entire U.S. Congress, Britain's Prince Charles, and dozens of leaders who ruled the world for the final third of the twentieth century.

The coffin sat on a catafalque directly below the cathedral's central tower. As they passed by to deliver eulogies, President Bush, former Canadian prime minister Brian Mulroney, and former president George Bush each paused to bow.

Recalling all he had been taught while serving as Reagan's vice president, the elder Bush fought back tears. "I learned kindness, we all did. I also learned courage, the nation did. I learned decency," he said, recalling a story of Reagan, still recovering from the 1981 assassination attempt, kneeling to wipe spilled water from the hospital floor so his nurse wouldn't get in trouble.

Mulroney remembered Reagan's devotion to his "beloved, indispensable Nancy." Former British prime minister Margaret Thatcher—who, weakened by strokes, attended the service but delivered a taped tribute—noted Reagan's dedication to "the great cause . . . of cheering us all up."

The service, which wove together moments of humor and sorrow, as well as several grace notes, had been planned by the former president himself in the years before he succumbed to Alzheimer's.

Supreme Court Justice Sandra Day O'Connor—appointed by Reagan as the court's first female member—read from a sermon by pilgrim John Winthrop that included the line: "We shall be as a city upon a hill," referenced by Reagan in his last speech from the Oval Office.

The grand scale of the cathedral and the passage of time rendered some larger-than-life figures small and frail. Chief Justice William H. Rehnquist shuffled slowly across the cathedral floor. Former Reagan defense secretary Caspar Weinberger greeted most well-wishers from his seat.

The scene provided a striking tableau of former presidents sitting together, some who admired Reagan, like Gerald R. Ford, others who challenged him. Jimmy Carter, defeated by Reagan in 1980, listened as Thatcher implicitly criticized his administration.

But even more than politics, the sight captured the mortality those men share—all but Bill Clinton have filed their own plans for a state funeral at the same cathedral.

The Armed Forces Chorus performed "The Battle Hymn of the Republic," one of the former president's favorites. Irish tenor Ronan Tynan sang "Amazing Grace." At exactly 1:00 P.M., as the cathedral bells rang forty times to honor the fortieth president, the coffin began its trek to Andrews Air Force Base, where another 3,000 observers waited.

Mrs. Reagan, wearing eyeglasses now and looking unsteady, paused before boarding the presidential jet to wave broadly at the crowd and blow a kiss. Then the plane departed in the last of what were once countless commutes from Washington, where he worked, to the Western vistas of home in California.

A bit less grand but no less touching, Reagan's California homecoming was a tardier affair, slowed by tens of thousands of well-wishers who lined the roads to pay their respects as the funeral cortege passed en route to the presidential library.

At 4:30 P.M., there was applause as Air Force One swept low over the Reagan library before landing at Point Mugu. Reagan's casket arrived at the library about 6:30 P.M., and the service began about twenty minutes later.

"We have come from sea to shining sea to this soil which he loved so much and where his body will remain," the Reverend Michael Wenning, retired senior pastor at Reagan's Bel Air Presbyterian Church, said in opening the ceremony.

Almost 700 guests attended the burial services, including Thatcher, California governor Arnold Schwarzenegger, and former California governors Pete Wilson and George Deukmejian.

The movie and television industries were represented by producer Norman Lear and actors Mickey Rooney, Kirk Douglas, Bo Derek, and Tom Selleck. Singers Johnny Mathis and entertainer Wayne Newton were there.

Selleck said Reagan would have been touched by the enormous outpouring of respect, admiration, and affection. "Suppose you throw a party and nobody comes?" Selleck said in an interview. "Well, everybody has come to this one."

Cannons fired a 21-gun salute. A bugler played taps. Fighter jets flew overhead in a traditional missing-man formation.

The flag that had draped the former president's coffin was folded by military pallbearers

After being flown across the country from Washington, D.C., former President Reagan's remains are laid on a bier by a military honor guard during the burial ceremony at the Ronald Reagan Presidential Library in Simi Valley, California, June 11, 2004.

and presented to Mrs. Reagan. She pressed her cheek to the coffin, speaking softly, caressing the polished wood with her hand. The president's children stood beside her, embracing her and offering their support.

Ronald Wilson Reagan, the fortieth president of the United States, said son Ron, "is home now, he is free."

Fiore and Kemper reported from Washington and Kelley from Simi Valley. Times *staff writers Elizabeth Shogren in Washington, Eric Malnic in Los Angeles, and Maria L. La Ganga in San Francisco contributed to this report.*

REMARKS BY PRESIDENT GEORGE H. W. BUSH IN EULOGY FOR PRESIDENT REAGAN

President Ronald Wilson Reagan's memorial service
at the National Cathedral, Washington, D.C.

hen Franklin Roosevelt died in 1945, *The New York Times* wrote: "Men will thank God 100 years from now that Franklin D. Roosevelt was in the White House."

It will not take 100 years to thank God for Ronald Reagan. But why? Why was he so admired? Why was he so beloved?

He was beloved, first, because of what he was.

Politics can be cruel, uncivil. Our friend was strong and gentle.

Once he called America hopeful, big-hearted, idealistic, daring, decent, and fair. That was America and, yes, our friend.

And next, Ronald Reagan was beloved because of what he believed. He believed in America, so he made it his shining city on a hill. He believed in freedom so he acted on behalf of its values and ideals. He believed in tomorrow, so the great communicator became the great liberator.

He talked of winning one for the Gipper, and as president, through his relationship with Mikhail Gorbachev . . . the Gipper, and yes, Mikhail Gorbachev won one for peace around the world.

If Ronald Reagan created a better world for many millions, it was because of the world someone else created for him.

Nancy was there for him always.

Her love for him provided much of his strength, and their love together transformed all of us as we've seen—renewed seeing again here in the last few days.

And one of the many memories we all have of both of them is the comfort they provided during our national tragedies.

Whether it was the families of the crew of the *Challenger* shuttle or the USS *Stark* or the Marines killed in Beirut, we will never forget those images of the president and first lady embracing them and embracing us during times of sorrow.

So, Nancy, I want to say this to you: Today America embraces you. We open up our arms. We seek to comfort you, to tell you of our admiration for your courage and your selfless caring.

And to the Reagan kids—it's OK for me to say that at eighty—Michael, Ron, Patti, today all of our sympathy, all of our condolences to you, and remember, too, your sister Maureen home safe now with her father.

As his vice president for eight years, I learned more from Ronald Reagan than from anyone I encountered in all my years of public life. I learned kindness; we all did.

April 28, 1981: Four weeks after the attempt on his life, President Reagan appears before a joint session of Congress. The president accepts the applause of Congress watched by Vice President George Bush and Speaker Tip O'Neill

I also learned courage; the nation did. Who can forget the horrible day in March 1981, he looked at the doctors in the emergency room and said, "I hope you're all Republicans."

And then I learned decency; the whole world did. Days after being shot, weak from wounds, he spilled water from a sink, and entering the hospital room, aides saw him on his hands and knees wiping water from the floor.

He worried that his nurse would get in trouble.

The Good Book says humility goes before honor, and our friend had both, and who could not cherish such a man?

And perhaps as important as anything, I learned a lot about humor, a lot about laughter. And oh, how President Reagan loved a good story. When asked, "How did your visit go with Bishop Tutu?" he replied, "So-so." It was typical. It was wonderful.

And in leaving the White House, the very last day, he left in the yard outside the Oval Office door a little sign for the squirrels. He loved to feed those squirrels. And he left this sign that said, "Beware of the dog," and to no avail, because our dog Millie came in and beat the heck out of the squirrels.

But anyway, he also left me a note, at the top of which said: "Don't let the turkeys get you down."

Well, he certainly never let them get him down. And he fought hard for his beliefs.

He led from conviction, but never made an adversary into an enemy. He was never mean-spirited.

Reverend Billy Graham, whom I refer to as the nation's pastor, is now hospitalized and regrets that he can't be here today. And I asked him for a Bible passage that might be appropriate. He suggested this from Psalm 37: "The Lord delights in the way of the man whose steps he has made firm. Though he stumble, he will not fall for the Lord upholds him with his hand."

And then this, too, from 37: "There is a future for the man of peace." God bless you, Ronald Wilson Reagan, and the nation you loved and led so well.

Lessons from Ronald Reagan

by Bob Schieffer,
chief Washington correspondent

———

We spent all week thinking about Ronald Reagan, and that was a good thing. He was our president for eight years. He helped restore our national confidence when it was fading. When he left Washington, we didn't understand that the Soviet Union was so near collapse. Now we can see how the policy he put in place helped to bring down an enemy that for nearly half a century had the means to destroy us and all civilization. Reason enough to remember him.

But there is one more thing to think about. This week of tribute to Ronald Reagan was a refreshing respite in a presidential campaign that began too soon and has grown increasingly bitter when the country is already more polarized than ever. What Reagan showed us, what today's politicians would do well to remember, is that it is possible to have differences without hating those on the other side; that winning an argument does not have to mean destroying your opponent. Somehow that's been lost in today's mean politics. Years of negative campaigns conducted almost exclusively by thirty-second television ads have gridlocked our political process and made the compromises necessary to govern all but impossible. Worse, it has soured our politics to the point that too many people no longer want anything to do with it.

The lesson from Ronald Reagan is that his way did work. If our politicians would remember only that about him, the level of our political dialogue would rise and campaigns would again become interesting, perhaps even relevant to solving the problems of our times.

Time, June 14, 2004

How His Legacy Lives On

by Richard Lacayo and John F. Dickerson

R onald Reagan utterly remade the American political land-scape. Even Bill Clinton, as adroit a politician as America has known, had to conduct his entire presidency in the confined political space in which Reagan placed him. It was because of Reagan that Clinton had to promise to end welfare as we know it. It was because of Reagan that he spoke the fateful line "The era of Big Government is over."

As it happens, it wasn't over—more on that later—but make no mistake, what Reagan brought forth was a revolution all the same. Like the Civil War and the New Deal, the Reagan years were another of those hinges upon which history sometimes turns. On one side, a wounded but still vigorous liberalism with its faith in government as the answer to almost every question. On the other, a free market so triumphant—even after the tech bubble burst—that we look first to "growth," not government, to solve most problems. On one side, a U.S. still licking its wounds from Vietnam, reluctant to exercise its power. On the other, U.S. forces in Bosnia, Haiti, Afghanistan, and Iraq. On one side, Russians invading Kabul. On the other, McDonald's invading Moscow.

Reagan was without a doubt the greatest communicator among postwar presidents. Even JFK, with his faintly patrician manner, could not play the effortless everyman as Reagan did. Every politician with national ambitions today tries to capture his easy way and Teflon character. All Republican candidates are conditioned now to always ask themselves, What would Reagan do?

He not only knew how to talk. He also knew how to use the power of his persuasion. "Reagan fundamentally changed the way the president and Congress relate," says Al From, former

Former president Reagan speaks at the Republican National Convention at the Astrodome in Houston on August 17, 1992.

head of the Democratic Leadership Council, which pushed the Democratic Party toward the center—inspired partly by Reagan's success in pushing the GOP to the right. "Before Reagan, if you wanted to get a big idea through Congress, you worked through the leadership. Reagan couldn't do that. The most important leader in Congress, House Speaker Tip O'Neill, was his enemy. So he figured out he had to go to the people. To get a big idea through Congress now, you go outside. Reagan understood that."

Ever since Reagan's departure from the political stage, GOP candidates have been trying to summon his image and perform the magic of uniting their party's disparate factions, from libertarians to religious conservatives to Big Business, under one tent. Don't forget that Reagan also left that imprint on another charismatic actor who now sits in the governor's chair in California. As he tries to find his way out of a nasty fiscal crisis, Arnold Schwarzenegger is taking lessons from the Reagan playbook all the time. "They both have extraordinary personal charm," observes Ken Khachigian, Reagan's former chief speechwriter. "That goes a great way in taking the sting out of things when you're doing something negative."

Remarkably, Reagan accomplished that while being the most conservative president his party had ever moved into the White House. Make no mistake. By Republican standards, Richard Nixon was middle of the road. He believed his job was not to dismantle the New Deal but to manage it more effectively than the Democrats did. And by those lights, Gerald Ford was no better, naming the ur-moderate Nelson Rockefeller, the bogeyman of the Republican right, his vice president.

"Reagan took a more moderate Republican Party and made it very conservative," says Larry Sabato, a political science professor at the University of Virginia. "Goldwater tried and failed to do that. Reagan succeeded." More than that, Reagan took who was next in line of Republican centrism, George H. W. Bush, vanquished him in the 1980 primaries, and then cordially digested him into his own administration. It was a lesson George the Younger never forgot.

So great was Reagan's victory in making his preoccupations into enduring themes of the national conversation that it may not matter that his record didn't always match his rhetoric. He insisted, for instance, that a balanced budget was one of his priorities. But by the time Reagan left office, a combination of lower tax revenues and sharply higher spending for defense had sent the deficit through the roof. But as Dick Cheney is reported to have said, "Reagan proved that deficits don't matter." In his recent memoir, former Bush treasury secretary Paul O'Neill quotes the vice president using those words to shut down an internal White House debate over the budgetary impact of Bush's tax cuts. And at least with respect to the political costs, he was right. Reagan demonstrated that among voters, the easily understood appeal of tax cuts neutralized the abstract peril of big deficits. It's a trick that the current administration is hoping can still be managed.

Yet if Reagan never balanced the budget, he changed the conversation about government. He made nonmilitary federal spending seem like an indulgence. Because of his two electoral landslides, a badly humbled Democratic Party had to think, really think, about reinventing government, trying free-market approaches to problems like public housing and health care that they once saw chiefly as targets for tax dollars. Four years after Reagan left office, the enduring popularity of his ideas obliged Clinton to back away from his 1993 stimulus spending package in favor of a budget more agreeable to the bond markets. When Clinton's proposed health plan started looking like a return to big government, voters rose up to produce

President Reagan's national security advisor General Colin Powell talks about the president at Reagan's eighty-fifth birthday celebrations at Chasen's restaurant in West Hollywood, California, on February 6, 1996. Reagan was unable to attend the event himself.

the '94 Republican sweep of Congress. By May of that year, only 2 percent of Americans were telling pollsters they had "a lot" of confidence that the federal government could tackle a problem and solve it. Two percent.

That '94 sweep was itself a delayed tremor of the Reagan upheaval. Newt Gingrich's Contract with America drew heavily from Reagan's legacy. But there was another lesson of Reaganism that Gingrich and the Republican class of '94 grasped too late: keep smiling. Even when his views were most intransigent—when he wondered out loud whether Martin Luther King, Jr., was a communist or failed for nearly all of his presidency to speak the word AIDS even once—Reagan gave Reaganism a human face. "He made us sunny optimists," says Bush political adviser Karl Rove. "His was a conservatism of laughter and openness and community."

By the nineties most presidential campaigners had learned to follow that model, and the ones who hadn't, like Pat Buchanan, crashed and burned in their own rhetorical fires. Bob Dole used to proclaim himself "the most optimistic man in America." And Clinton was the Reagan of the liberals, always full of bright-faced hope for a new tomorrow. By comparison, Gingrich and his followers made conservatism look snide and angry and strenuous. They learned the phrases but never the genial delivery of the man who carried forty-nine states in 1984 without breaking a sweat.

That's a mistake George W. Bush has been careful not to repeat. Though he ran in 2000 on a platform as hard-edged as any president's since, well, Reagan's, he was careful to style himself that year as a "compassionate conservative." One of Bush's recent campaign commercials—a girl watches her father raising an American flag as a narrator assures us that "America is turning the corner"—could be an outtake from Reagan's famous 1984 "Morning in America" campaign.

The Bush White House has absorbed the lessons of Reagan-era foreign policy, too. From the first, Reagan moved aggressively to undo the "Vietnam syndrome," the postwar hesitation to project American power by force and to act unilaterally in places like Libya and Grenada. These days, when we do that in Iraq, we call it the Bush doctrine. But Reagan also presided over a moment of weakness that led America's enemies in the Middle East to believe that terrorism could work. On October 23, 1983, Hizballah terrorists blew up Marine barracks in Beirut, killing 241. A few months later, Reagan withdrew the remaining U.S. forces. Two decades after that, National Security Advisor Condoleezza Rice put it this way: "Prior to September 11, our policies as a nation, going really all the way back to the bombing of the Lebanon barracks, were not in a mode of the kind of war that we were fighting." Translation: We cut and ran. Terrorists drew their own conclusions.

The White House may return to the Democrats some day. Even Congress may go back their way. But the federal courts will be Reagan's for years to come. He named 83 appeals-court judges and 292 district-court judges, slightly more than half the federal judiciary. That's more federal judges named than by any other president in history.

Reagan's impact on the judiciary has been profound. Federal courts today are far more willing to question racial and ethnic preferences. Mandatory busing for school desegregation is now a museum piece. Court rulings in criminal cases are far more likely to favor law enforcement. Laws once prohibited even moments of silence in classrooms and remedial education for the underprivileged in sectarian schools. Now school vouchers for use in private schools, both secular and sectarian, hold up in courts.

The real Reagan years, the years of red suspenders and corporate takeovers, of *Bonfire of the Vanities* and big hair, were shorter than they seem in memory. They began around the middle of his first term, after the 1981 recession gave way to the boom years, and ended midway through his second, when Iran-contra broke and so in some ways did Reagan's spell. But however briefly they lasted, those years habituated us to a giddy, swaggering, saw-toothed capitalism that seemed a bit appalling then. It feels much more familiar now. Because the country had lived through the eighties, through all those poison pills and hostile takeovers and Donald Trump, the unapologetic materialism of the nineties—the stock options and IPOs, the $21 soup courses and twenty-two-year-old millionaires (and Donald Trump!)—seemed more like business as usual in the most literal sense of the words.

But it won't do to end by emphasizing a Reagan legacy of unintended consequences. The consequences he wanted—an America that is stronger militarily, more dedicated to free enterprise, more mindful of the virtues of self-reliance, and more confident in its own powers—were the ones he got as well, and the ones he passed on firmly to America. Ronald Reagan may be gone, but will it ever be accurate to call this nation "post-Reagan"?

The Washington Post, June 8, 2004

A PARADOX

by Richard Cohen

Back in 1984 I wrote about the travails of being a twin—about how I never got to have my own birthday and how things had recently gotten even worse because, as it happened, Ronald Reagan had also been born on February 6. Soon afterward I was feverishly scribbling up an anti-Reagan screed when a telegram arrived from Air Force One—a birthday greeting, graceful and witty, from a sympathetic Ronald and Nancy Reagan. The screed would have to wait for another day.

That aspect of Reagan—his niceness, his graciousness, and his indomitable good humor—has been much remarked on since the fortieth president died, and so I will not bore you with more of the same. I'd just like to

say, though, that these qualities—and all they represented—transformed the modern presidency. After Reagan, politicians everywhere tried to be Reagan.

This is not the time to quibble about Reagan's place in history, such as whether he single-handedly ended the cold war. It is the time, though, to acknowledge he was right about the Soviet Union—it was the evil empire—and about welfare abuses and the occasional arrogant insularity of big government. On certain issues, he had been intellectually courageous for breaking with the liberal orthodoxy of Hollywood and his own past.

Above all, Reagan was very much a paradoxical figure. He was famously genial but impossible to know well. He could be astoundingly ignorant about the basic facts of government or policy—both in Sacramento and Washington— and he could create his own world, not just as a movie actor but also as a public figure. He sometimes confused fiction with fact, simply, I think, because he preferred life to have three acts, the last ending in a magnificent sunset. He was not just an optimist. He was a fabulist.

This was Reagan's most important—and characteristic— paradox and, in a way, his gift. When he declared his candidacy for California governor, he was derided as nothing but an actor—and a B one at that. (To their regret, Jimmy Carter's campaign aides held the same view.) But Reagan knew better. In a television age, there is no such thing as a mere actor. It is the most invaluable experience a politician can have.

Reagan understood that. But he understood—or felt— something else as well: the camera does not lie. It's not merely that it captures reality but that it delves into the soul. He was convinced that if you liked someone on the screen you would like him in person—that the camera reveals personality and character. He knew, based on success in the movies, that he had both. And he knew, too, that his movie and public-speaking careers had given him the tools—call it artifice, if you will—to exhibit those qualities.

Television allowed Reagan to revert to an older style of

leadership, when a commander faced his troops and exhorted them in person. The qualities of leadership that once were exhibited to a small group could, with television, be extended infinitely. Of course, Reagan was too skilled to shout or declaim. His version of Henry V's St. Crispin's Day speech ("We few, we happy few, we band of brothers") would have been said softly. FDR understood the power of radio, and Reagan understood the much greater power of television.

During Reagan's 1984 reelection campaign, for instance, Lesley Stahl of CBS did a long (four-minute) piece about his contradictions. She showed him appearing at old-age homes and institutions for the handicapped, and then noted that he had reduced funding for those programs. Afterward, the White House thanked her for the piece. The pictures were terrific. They were all that mattered.

One other paradox: Reagan was a cottage industry for biographers and others who sought to plumb his depths. His inner self mattered, we were told, and so too did his lackadaisical parenting. But watching television over the weekend, I found myself not caring. Time sifts the petty from the grand. Abraham Lincoln had a difficult marriage. It matters more—it matters only—that Lincoln preserved the union.

For a long time now, I've found myself thinking of Reagan—perplexed by him, wondering about him, envisioning him in the spongy grip of Alzheimer's. This is the final paradox. I opposed much of what he did and much of what he tried to do—Star Wars, for instance. But he nonetheless came to mind every February 6, and he was welcome.

Like you, I knew him well. And like you, I did not know him at all.

The New York Times, June 11, 2004

LEGACY OF REAGAN NOW BEGINS THE TEST OF TIME

by R. W. Apple, Jr.

Franklin D. Roosevelt once defined great presidents as those who were "leaders of thought at times when certain ideas in the life of the nation had to be clarified."

By that reckoning and most others, Roosevelt himself earned a place on the list of greats for rallying the nation in the Depression and leading it to the brink of victory in World War II. Washington, who bent to the hard work of nation-building; Lincoln, who saved the union; and Jefferson, who codified some of its ideals, are other universal choices. Not by coincidence, all four have monuments in Washington.

But what of Ronald Reagan, whose weeklong farewell ceremonies, culminating on Friday in a funeral at the National Cathedral and burial in California, have stirred such emotion and such largely laudatory comment? What will history, with its privileged vantage point far from the heat of partisan battles, conclude about him?

Clearly, Mr. Reagan died a respected, perhaps even a beloved man, although the affection was far from universal, as is true for any public figure. In office, his popularity, though dented, survived the Iran-contra affair, but popularity is never a reliable test of greatness.

President Reagan on Air Force One, June 1986.

Harry S. Truman, now counted among the near greats if not the greats, retrospectively admired for his prosecution of the cold war, left office with an approval rating of only 23 percent. Warren G. Harding, now disdained, whose stated ambition was to be remembered as the country's "best-loved president," came close to that goal after his sudden death in 1923.

It could be argued that Mr. Reagan's greatest triumphs came in his role as chief of state rather than as chief of government. He was often ignorant of or impatient with the policy minutiae that preoccupy most occupants of the Oval Office, sometimes with unfortunate consequences (as when Oliver North ran amok in the Iran-contra affair, for instance). But his extraordinary political gifts carried him through—his talents as a communicator, his intuitive understanding of the average American, his unfailing geniality even after being hit by a would-be assassin's bullet, his ability to build and sustain friendships across partisan lines (as with Tip O'Neill, for instance).

Those gifts—and his conviction that words counted for far more in politics than mere deeds—enabled him to convince large majorities that as long as he was in charge, it would remain "Morning in America." They made it possible for him to redraw the nation's political map, moving the center so abruptly to the right that even Bill Clinton would proclaim the end of big government, and to remold his party in his own image. They gave him the eloquence to lead the country

TOP: The fortieth anniversary of D-day, the allied invasion of France, was celebrated in June 1984. The Reagans visited the graves of some of the American troops killed during the fierce fighting on Omaha Beach in Normandy.

ABOVE: The president and first lady meeting Pope John Paul II at the Vatican, June 1982.

in mourning after the *Challenger* disaster and to celebrate "the boys of Pointe du Hoc" near Omaha Beach on the fortieth anniversary of D-day.

Vice President Dick Cheney hailed Mr. Reagan as "a graceful and a gallant man," and more than that, "a providential man" who provided precisely what the nation and the world needed at a crucial moment.

"But he was not a great president," said Sean Wilentz, professor of history at Princeton University, who was a vocal opponent of Mr. Clinton's impeachment in 1998. "He was master at projecting a mood; he could certainly rally the country. He would have made a great king, a great constitutional monarch, but we do not have that form of government."

Success in war underpins the claims to greatness of many presidents. Jackson wins the plaudits of historians for broadening the character of American democracy by extending the franchise. But he was a celebrated soldier long before he became president, as were Washington, Theodore Roosevelt, and Dwight D. Eisenhower, whose standing among historians and other commentators has increased markedly since he left office. Lincoln, FDR, Truman, and James K. Polk (the victor in the Mexican War) were all wartime commanders in chief.

Mr. Reagan spent World War II, the global conflict fought and won by his gen-

TOP: Presidents Ford, Reagan, Carter, and Nixon in the White House Blue Room before leaving for Egypt for the funeral of President Anwar Sadat, October 1981.

ABOVE: Five presidents and their wives attended the funeral service of former President Richard Nixon in Yorba Linda, California, April 27, 1994. Left to right: Bill and Hillary Clinton; George and Barbara Bush; Ronald and Nancy Reagan; Jimmy and Rosalynn Carter; and Gerald and Betty Ford.

eration, making training films in Hollywood. But he came to power as the cold war was nearing a denouement, and he did all he could to hasten the process by beefing up the American military and then, in Berlin, boldly challenging Soviet leaders to "tear down this wall." After that, it would have been hard for Mikhail S. Gorbachev to believe that Americans had lost their will to resist Soviet power, and he joined with Mr. Reagan to bring the long struggle to a conclusion. It was the result of forty-five years of aggressive allied containment, but the commander in chief, as always, got much of the credit.

Without doubt, that will form a very important part of Mr. Reagan's legacy, as one aspect of his vision. In his book *Hail to the Chief: The Making and Unmaking of American Presidents* (Hyperion, 1996), the historian Robert Dallek lists vision as a sine qua non of presidential greatness, along with "pragmatism, ability to achieve consensus, charisma, and trustworthiness." Few will deny Mr. Reagan's trustworthiness or his immense charisma, matched only in the modern era by FDR and John F. Kennedy, and he demonstrated his pragmatism in rolling back some of his huge 1981 tax cuts with two tax increases when the cuts failed to produce as much revenue as he expected.

Mr. Reagan had another vision, but he fell well short of the "ability to produce consensus" behind it, then or now. Much of the country, including most of those who are physically, economically, or otherwise disadvantaged, deeply resented and still resent his insistence that government is the problem, not the solution. Severe and continuing cutbacks in government services to the poor and vulnerable resulted, and the gulf dividing rich from poor widened.

If Mr. Reagan's celebrated optimism lifted the veil of malaise that darkened the Jimmy Carter era, it also obscured major problems. Many missed Mr. Carter's burning commitment to civil rights and liberties at home and human rights abroad. African-Americans and trade union members felt

particularly aggrieved, as did many Jews, who resented Mr. Reagan's participation in a ceremony in 1985 at a German cemetery where Nazi SS troopers were buried.

To some degree, history's verdict is shaped by the values of the time in which that history is written, and whom it is written by. H. L. Mencken, ever wary of pompous speeches and empty promises, rated Calvin Coolidge highly because, as he once wrote: "There were no thrills while he reigned, but neither were there any headaches. He had no ideas, and he was not a nuisance."

Reputation is also shaped by perspective. A group of American and Australian political figures and others, assembled in Washington for a conference this week, disagreed sharply on Woodrow Wilson—the foreigners called him a flop, largely because of his rigid and eventually counterproductive idealism, while the Americans (like most historians) held him in higher esteem. Historians may say that Kennedy held office for too short a time to achieve true greatness in the presidency, but for many around the globe he still embodies the best of the United States, which is why there are streets named for him and pictures of him hanging in houses all over the world.

So far at least, Mr. Reagan has achieved no such status overseas, although as president he was held in far more esteem in Europe than George W. Bush is. His brand of radical conservatism had a counterpart in Britain under Margaret Thatcher, but it has achieved little success elsewhere.

Some presidents leave behind records so contradictory as to cloud generalization. Richard M. Nixon's foreign-policy achievements, most significantly his rapprochement with Beijing, were eclipsed in his final years in office by domestic-policy failings and his evident shortcomings as a moral leader. Vietnam blackened Lyndon B. Johnson's reputation and forced him from office, despite his tremendous achievements in domestic policy, notably in lifting the cruel yoke of segregation from black Americans.

It is not entirely clear yet what those two presidents will most be remembered for—what one achievement or failure will attach to their names, at least in popular history, as the crusade against the trusts, the "malefactors of great wealth," attaches to Teddy Roosevelt's, and Credit Mobilier

In March 1992, the Reagans celebrated their fortieth wedding anniversary by renewing their vows at a private ceremony. This is an official photograph commemorating the occasion.

and other scandals attach to Ulysses S. Grant's, all but wiping out his role as a war hero.

The "Reaganauts," as one of them said, have been out all week seeking to burnish their man's legacy on television and in print. But hagiography will not determine their leader's ultimate standing, and whether he is entitled to be called "great." Only what the historian Arthur M. Schlesinger, Jr., called "the cool eye of history" will do that, many years hence.

RONALD REAGAN

Nov. 5, 1994

My Fellow Americans,

I have recently been told that I am one of the millions of Americans who will be afflicted with Alzheimer's Disease.

Upon learning this news, Nancy & I had to decide whether as private citizens we would keep this a private matter or whether we would make this news known in a public way.

In the past Nancy suffered from breast cancer and I had my cancer surgeries. We found through our open disclosures we were able to raise public awareness. We were happy that as a result many more people underwent testing. They were treated in early stages and able to return to normal, healthy lives.

So now, we feel it is important to share it with you. In opening our hearts, we hope this might promote greater awareness of this condition. Perhaps it will encourage a clearer understanding of the individuals and families who are affected by it.

At the moment I feel just fine. I intend to live the remainder of the years God gives me on this earth doing the things I have always done. I will continue to share life's journey with my beloved Nancy and my family. I plan to enjoy the great outdoors and stay in touch with my friends and supporters.

Unfortunately, as Alzheimer's Disease progresses, the family often bears a heavy burden. I only wish there was some way I could spare Nancy from this painful experience. When the time comes I am confident that with your help she will face it with faith and courage.

In closing let me thank you, the American people for giving me the great honor of allowing me to serve as your President. When the Lord calls me home, whenever that may be, I will leave with the greatest love for this country of ours and eternal optimism for its future.

I now begin the journey that will lead me into the sunset of my life. I know that for America there will always be a bright dawn ahead.

Thank you my friends. May God always bless you.

Sincerely,
Ronald Reagan

EPILOGUE: RONALD REAGAN'S ALZHEIMER'S LETTER, NOVEMBER 5, 1994

On November 5, 1994, Ronald Reagan released a letter announcing that he had been diagnosed with Alzheimer's disease. Following is a facsimile of the handwritten letter and its text. With the letter, Reagan began what he described as "the journey that will lead me into the sunset of my life." President Reagan died on June 5, 2004.

My Fellow Americans,

I have recently been told that I am one of the millions of Americans who will be afflicted with Alzheimer's disease.

Upon learning this news, Nancy and I had to decide whether as private citizens we would keep this a private matter or whether we would make this news known in a public way.

In the past Nancy suffered from breast cancer and I had my cancer surgeries. We found through our open disclosures we were able to raise public awareness. We are happy that as a result many more people underwent testing.

They were treated in early stages and able to return to normal, healthy lives.

So now, we feel it is important to share it with you. In opening our hearts, we hope this might promote greater awareness of this condition. Perhaps it will encourage a clearer understanding of the individuals and families who are affected by it.

At the moment I feel just fine. I intend to live the remainder of the years God gives me on this earth doing the things I have always done. I will con-

tinue to share life's journey with my beloved Nancy and my family. I plan to enjoy the great outdoors and stay in touch with my friends and supporters.

Unfortunately, as Alzheimer's disease progresses, the family often bears a heavy burden. I only wish there was some way I could spare Nancy from this painful experience. When the time comes I am confident that with your help she will face it with faith and courage.

In closing let me thank you, the American people, for giving me the great honor of allowing me to serve as your President. When the Lord calls me home, whenever that may be, I will leave with the greatest love for this country of ours and eternal optimism for its future.

I now begin the journey that will lead me into the sunset of my life. I know that for America there will always be a bright new dawn ahead.

Thank you, my friends. May God always bless you.

Sincerely,
Ronald Reagan